Starting A Freelance Writing Business

John E Derossett

CONTENTS

ACKNOWLEDGMENTS

I want to extend a personal thank you to everyone behind the scenes who helped to make this book possible including Beta Readers, Editors and those who helped to research data for the book. There are far too many people to name individually and I apologize for that, but you know who you are!

THE STARTUP

FREELANCING DEFINED

In its simplest form, the definition of a freelancer is a person who works for themselves, performing services for a company or another individual. Freelancing services are offered in a number of different fields including writing, photography, web design, programming or virtually any other type of service for that matter.

The most significant difference between having a regular writing job and freelance writing, is the fact that you will be writing for many people or companies, instead of just one. Another term for those who work in the freelance field is contractor. Many companies will call you a contractor if you work for them sporadically, for a set fee. It's beneficial to the company, because they are not responsible to the government for paying employment taxes and fringe benefits when you are a contractor. In fact, they can in many cases, save as much as 75% in overhead costs when they hire a freelancer as opposed to having a full time employee on the payroll. That's the primary reason there has been such significant growth in the freelance industry over the last few years.

While many freelancers consider the work as having a different type of job, and it is, but the reality is that as a freelancer, you are now running your own business, and you have to treat it as such. We will go into detail later on in this book, but just start thinking about the fact that you are now going to have to track all of your income (naturally), as well as any money that you spend during the course of conducting business. There are certain deductions that will be able to take at the end of the tax year to increase your actual income, or the "bottom line", but again, we'll talk more about that later on in the book.

Now, there are certain freedoms that come along with freelance writing as your career. That's where the beauty of the job comes into play. For instance, as a writer, you will be working from home, or you can set up an office somewhere to go to, or you can travel to your grandma's house (assuming an internet connection) and work from there just the same as you could if you went into an office every day.

When you are operating your own business, the benefits are great, but you have to remember that unlike working for someone else, where you will get paid the same thing whether you are actually performing a task or not, as a freelancer, you will usually be paid for only the words you write. Anything else that you have to do in-between is "dead time". Simply put, the time you are putting into actually writing words for you clients, is when you are making money, and anytime that you are doing anything else, there is no income being generated.

That said, freelancing can be a struggle at times. That's why I mentioned in the introduction that you should be saving money when the work is flush, for those times when the work projects are few. Freelancing offers many great rewards, but just like anything else, there is a cost attached to those rewards. That means if you fail to save, then the times when there are few, or even no clients (and there WILL be times when there are no clients), then you will sink quickly.

I am supposing that you have already decided that what you would really like to do is to become a freelance writer. Otherwise, you would not have purchased this book. If you put the effort into the venture, you WILL reap those rewards, and enjoy sitting at home (or anywhere else for that matter), while everyone else is fighting the daily grind in rush-hour traffic, or riding commuter trains trying to get to the office so that they can make other people rich with their efforts.

YOUR "REGULAR" JOB

The first thing that you need to think about is whether you will start out freelancing full-time or part-time. If you are already unemployed for whatever reason, this is a no-brainer. Likewise, if you already have the resources to sustain your chosen way of life without going to a job outside the home, then you probably already have your answer to the issue. If you depend on a job outside the home to pay your monthly expenses however, then I suggest that you start out part-time and then build your business by working on freelance writing during the off hours from your regular job.

Once you reach the point where your freelance income, minus all expenses exceed the take-home pay from your job, then you can consider leaving the regular job safely, financially speaking.

When I actually dove into freelancing, I was already involved in an online business - Internet Gambling. I didn't take bets or anything like that, rather, I built portals packed with gambling information, tips, tricks, etc, and posted affiliate ads from online casinos on the site. It took some time to build, but grow it did. Eventually I bought a forum from a friend of mine, and it grew. The casino affiliate programs sponsored the website and revenue in our company continued to grow.

When the United States decided to take a stand against online gambling, I decided to sell the forum and several websites to a company in Boston who also was in the gambling information business. We then took the proceeds, plus financing on our house and opened a retail store, exactly at the wrong time to do so. Ultimately, we closed the store in late 2007 and I was out of work with our home in foreclosure status. That's an entirely different story and not for these pages however. What I ended up with, was no job, no income and nothing else to lose, in a time when jobs were few and far in-between. I had no choice but to do something and that's when I got involved in freelance writing. In fact, it wasn't long before I was generating income or more than two thousand dollars per month, gross (about seven months).

If you are already working a regular job, keeping that while you test the freelancing waters can give you a chance to build your business without much risk. In fact, there are several distinct advantages to starting your freelancing company on a part-time basis.

ADVANTAGES

- **Testing the Market** - If you give up the security of your regular full-time job, you create a situation of fear inasmuch as making sure your bills are paid is concerned.If you keep your job however, then you actually give yourself the chance of building a clientele before leaving your regular job, ensuring that you have an income even after you leave the day job, as I like to call it. If you approach the business in this manner, and decide that it isn't for you for some reason, you can always back out of it without the penalty of sacrificing a regular income.
- **As a freelancer**, you can take all of the holidays that you want. The primary difference is that you will not be getting paid while you are not writing. On the other hand, there is no hassle or blackout dates when you want to take a vacation. Another way to view it though, is that while you are on vacation, you can still be making money while sitting by the pool sipping your Mai-Tais. HOWEVER, if you are still employed at another company, you will be paid for all holidays that they observe, and you can write or do whatever else you wish on that day, knowing that the pay envelope is going to be there at the end of the week.

- **Freelancing while you** are still employed by another company gives you the chance to build a client-base, ensuring regular future income, before you ever leave the day job. This also gives you an opportunity to build a nice portfolio of writing clips, which most clients will want to be able to view when considering hiring your for their project.
- **Finally, another thing** to consider is that building your business while still employed for another company, you will be able to build up a nice nestegg to fall back on should the work taper off for a while, and it does.

DISADVANTAGES

- There are some disadvantages to starting your freelancing business while employed by another company. The one that has the most importance with most people is that you will have less time for the extra things in life that are important, such as family time. Still, when you consider that one of the advantages is ultimately more free time in your life, this should actually be a minor problem. You have to schedule your time, and do everything that you can to schedule the things in your life that are important and this will actually make more time for family and friends, while still working both jobs. You have to keep in mind however, that it will not be easy, but only you can decide whether or not you can manage to make time for everything you want and need to do when building your business
- You will not be able to complete your freelance projects while at your day job. Even if you intend to do the work while on your lunch break or whatever, the reality is that trying to do that is not going to give your freelancing client 100% in their completed project. The absolute best thing to do is to leave your freelancing work wherever you normally do it, and to concentrate on your day job while there. Otherwise, the work on both jobs will suffer.

- Stress from your day job usually is lessened once you leave the company your work for that day. It's not going to be that easy when you start feeling the pressure from your freelancing business. This usually crops up when your workload is too much to handle easily. When you begin searching for freelance clients, only take on the number of projects that you know you can realistically complete within the required deadlines. Restricting yourself to part-time freelancing while still employed for another will help to keep the stress and nights of lost sleep to a minimum.

- As a freelance writer, part-time or otherwise, it's hard to click with clients. You will have clients who refuse to discuss business outside the typical 9 to 5 hours, and on weekends, while you may be working in the evenings and on weekends as well. On the other hand, you might have clients in different time zones who insist on being able to speak with you any time they wish. This of course is not fair to you because it begins cutting into your private life. That said, you can help to alleviate this problem by setting your own specific hours and adhering to them. While we do live in an age where "the customer is always right", customers also need to respect the fact that there is a necessity for private time.

- Loss of Sleep. This can also be an issue. It just depends on what your specific needs are. Make sure of course, that you schedule you available time for work and family so thatit does not interfere with your sleeping patterns.

PART-TIME JOB WHILE FREELANCING

I hit on this a little earlier in the book. There are times, and likely will continue to be times when you will require some income to supplement your freelance income. If you decide to go into freelancing full-time, then consider continuing in your day job part-time, or getting another part-time job as you are building your freelancing business. Like in the previous section, you will find advantages to having a part-time job while starting your freelancing company including:

- You can rest assured that you have income coming into your bank even if you currently have no writing clients.
- You have weekly, or bi-weekly reminders of exactly why you want to become a freelance writer in the first place.
- Working full-time can hinder or limit the amount of time you have available for writing. Working a part-time job will give you the extra time you need to concentrate on your freelance business while at the same time providing you with some income.
- The part-time job, much like the full-time job, gives you time to build a client-base. The primary difference is that if you are working another job only part-time, then you have more time to devote to your writing.

Now, just like there are advantages to working a part-time job while building your freelance business, there will also be some disadvantages. These disadvantages include:

- You tend to get too comfortable with free-time. It's important that you understand that you must work the hours you schedule yourself to be working when building a freelance writing business. If you are not actually writing because the workflow is low, then you need to be marketing yourself and seeking out new clientele. The only way you are going to grow your business is to stick with it.
- Your part-time job too, might drain your energy. Many employers will attempt to sway you away from the part-time schedule by asking you to come in more, or to leave later. You have to have the self-discipline to know the

limits where the freelance business is concerned. If you were hired to work say, twenty hours a week, and the boss asks you to come in more than that occasionally, that's fine, but you have to realized that if it happens all the time, it sort of defeats the purpose of having a part-time job while building your freelance business.

FREELANCING FULL-TIME

LET ME REITERATE ONCE AGAIN THAT I DO NOT RECOMMEND QUITTING YOUR FULL-TIME JOB TO START A NEW FREELANCING BUSINESS.

You need to learn the ins and outs of the business, and build a reliable client-base before you do, or you will soon find yourself in a precarious position. There are a few who have dove right into freelancing fulltime and have become very successful at it, but you have to understand that those people had skills that you may not yet have including strong writing skills, and the ability to market themselves because they are already experienced in marketing. Launching a full-time business in any field is a risky venture, at best, but if your resources are already limited, they will become even more so by just jumping in and hoping to sink or swim. Again, here are some advantages to jumping in full-time:

ADVANTAGES

- Giving up your free time is not necessary if you go into freelance writing full-time right away. Some people find having to work evenings and weekends to be a huge imposition. In fact, there are those who find that having to do that to build their freelance writing business that find it downright impossible. These people need plenty of time to recharge the batteries, and of course to spend time with their families. Jumping in full-time right away does not take this free time from them.
- You are available during what most clients feel are regular working hours (9 to 5), which of course, makes your

customers happier when they need to get in contact with you.

DISADVANTAGES

- Working alone, as you will likely be in the startup of your new business can be a daunting task for some, who like having others around when they are working. In fact, some people can and do become downright lonely. During this time, you may be tempted to turn on the television, nd indeed, I like to have some background noise when I am working, but just don't fall into the no-work pit and find yourself missing deadlines before you even have your new business established and making money. You will over time, develop the self-discipline necessary notto sway from what needs to be done, but don't fall into bad habits early on, or you will never develop that self-discipline you require.
- Let's not forget the financial risks that will constantly be looming around the corner until you are finally established and have customers looking for you to get the job done. You have to remember that once you establish your working hours, you have to actually be doing something during the work day. If you have no writing projects, spend the available time LOOKING for writing projects, and not seeing what's on the latest episode of Maury Povich.

LEAVING THE DAY JOB

At some point in time during the growth of your new freelancing business, you will find that it's time to quit working for others in order to concentrate on building your own business.

One thing that I recommend you do wholeheartedly, is that you leave the company you are working for on good terms. Until you are firmly establish in your new business, which realistically take a couple of years, despite the amount of money you are making,you may want to return to the company if something goes wrong.

Additionally, it is especially important to remain on good terms if the company is in the same field that you are going into, not to mention the opportunities that may open to you to write for the company blogs, or the blogs belonging to their clients.

STARTUP FUNDS

When you decide to embark on a career of freelance writing, there are certain things that you are going to need to get started, which means that yes, startup funds are required.In some cases, you may already nhaving the required equipment seeing how we are an electronics oriented society. Still, you must consider at least the minimum to start properly, which includes all of the following:

- Office equipment such as a desk, computer, printer, paper, software and other office supplies.
- The cost of an account or at the very least, an accounting program.
- Developing a company identity such as a logo, website, business cards and other such materials geared toward marketing your services.
- Reserve funds for operating expenses such as supply replenishment, etc. To have on hand in case sales do not come as quick as originally expected.

Frankly, is there no way of knowing exactly how much you will need for starting YOUR business. Only you know how much you are going to need based on the equipment that you may already have on hand. You need to grab yourself a pen and sheet of paper and make a list:

- List the expenses you will have by listing the equipment you are going to need. Each item should have its own line. Be sure to include things like business cards, promotional materials, paper, office supplies, etc.
- List your monthly household expenses and add those up and then multiply the final amount times three. Add that final sum to the total you will need for supplies and

equipment. This will equal the total startup amount you will need to jump into freelancing full-time.

Keep in mind that even the most experienced of freelancers will find it difficult to build a new freelance writing business.This does not necessarily have anything to do with knowledge or lack thereof, but more with outside forces. As the old saying goes: "Murphy's law says that if it can happen, it probably will happen". You have to plan ahead for anything that might happen to interrupt your income stream. If it never happens, great, but the chances are more favorable that some will come up and it's best to have a little nest egg set aside for just such an event.

As a matter of fact, it's always a good idea that you maintain some sort of savings, perhaps even up to three months of those aforementioned expenses, even when business is good. The bottom line, is even some of the so-called experts in the business world miss when it comes to predicting sales. Your business is small enough that you must be more diligent in watching trends, and making sure that you have enough reserve cash to get you through the rough patches.

ACCOUNTING AND LEGAL REQUIREMENTS

It doesn't matter what type of business you start - you are always going to have to meet accounting and legal requirements when it comes to business. Keep in mind that these requirements are written for the United States. The laws probably vary in your country, and it's up to you to use your due diligence to make sure you are handling everything in a legal manner based on the local laws where you live.

BUSINESS STRUCTURE

The first thing that you have to do is to choose your business structure. Most countries offer a variety of different ways you can structure your business for legal and tax purposes. The simplest form of business in the United States is the sole proprietorship.

With this type of business, you file taxes using form 1040 and schedule C, along with several other schedules if they apply to your business. Since you are also your own employer, you will have to file estimated quarterly self-employment taxes as well.

The corporation is another form of business in the U.S. If you choose this sort of business method, then you end up paying more taxes as you are essentially double-taxed since the corporation files and pays an income tax, and then you file and pay your personal income tax. This type of business removes liability of any lawsuits that might arise against the company, as long as you were doing nothing illegal in the process, however, there is a lot more involved than that simple statement. It's best to contact a business lawyer to discuss the types of business structures before you choose and register your business as such.

Next is the S corporation. This type of corporation is similar to the corporation, as it limits your liability for the debts of the company, provided you were doing nothing illegal, but in reality it Works by recording the income of the company, minus expenses, then the net profit passes through to you as income and you file a form (schedule K) with your personal taxes to claim the income.

The partnership is exactly as it sounds. Income is divided down the middle and split between the partners, as are the expenses. Income and expenses are then reported on the 1040 form along with schedule C and any other schedules that you may need.

Finally, there is the LLC which works much like a partnership, but allows for the limited liability of your personal assets should the company get sued for any reason.

Like I said, you have to use your due diligence and investigate every possibility. Consult a lawyer and tax accountant. For myself, based on what I already knew of business and such, I settled on the S corporation, but I AM NOT AN ATTORNEY. Make your choice based on your specific needs and the advice that you get from the professionals.

If you choose to conduct business as a sole proprietorship, you usually will not have to do anything as far as a business license is concerned if you are working out of your home and no customers will come to your door. This may differ in your state and it never hurts to call the local courthouse to find out. Remember, I AM NOT A LAWYER. You will however, usually have to register with the State to indicate to them that you are conducting business, so that they issue a Tax ID number to your company for the purpose of sales and use tax, personal property taxes for the business, etc. The clerk of the court in the area in which you live will be able to give you specific information in that aspect of your business. For the tax ID and information in that respect, you must call your local tax department, which is usually called the Comptroller of the Treasury.

The best option is to go to a local bank. There used to be a number of banks that done business online, and many still do, but with all of the fraud that goes on today, many of them want you to come into the office to open a business account so that they can see that you are really you. By establishing a business banking account, you achieve a couple of things. First, you separate your personal expense from business expenses. This is important. Second, you lend credibility to your business and people that you deal with see that you are serious about your new company. Third, as your business grows, you might want to establish business credit, and you will need a bank reference in most cases.

LAWYERS AND ACCOUNTANTS

The sooner you seek the advice of a lawyer and accountant, the better off you will be. The costs of these services are high, without a doubt, so it's always best to look for those who offer free initial consultations so that you can first find out what you need, and what it will cost if you need their services for anything. If you operate as a sole proprietor, you may not actually need their services at all. It depends, and everything is relative to your specific wants and needs. There's a lot to be said though, when you secure the services of a good accountant, who will be able to give you sound business advice where it relates to the financial matters of your company. He will also help to make sure that you only pay the bare minimum in taxes, meaning that you won't overpay, because frankly, the government is not inclined to tell you that you are sending too much. As for the startup of your business, your income and expenses are going to be simple enough to manage on your own. Especially if you use one of th many accounting programs available today. Come tax time though, you should enlist the help of a pro. You will simply be able to give them a copy of the printed reports from your accounting program, and they can take things from there.

THE BUSINESS PLAN

Regardless of the size of your business, a business plan is essential. There are software programs on the market that can help to make it easier to develop one, but frankly, some of the best business plans have been known to find their start on a simple sheet of paper. Spending a great deal of time is not necessary when developing the business plan. As long as the business plan spells out the direction that the business is starting out in, and pointing the direction that it needs to take, along with some financial planning, you will be fine. The fancy plans can come about later on, when you need to present it for financing or some other deal you are about to make.

The business plan itself is nothing more than a detailed summary of how you intend to establish your business, gain a client-base, and make money. It's as simple as that. The plan actually breaks down into two distinct sections, with a summary:

1. **The Marketing Plan** - This section should outline how you plan to obtain your clients and ultimately, getting them to hire you to complete the work they need done. It also generally spells out how you will advertise your business and it will ask you to establish goals. The marketing plan is

generally updated periodically as you meet your goals to establish new goals.

2. **The Financial Plan** - In this section, you will define what you will charge, how you will collect the money and what you expect cash flow to be throughout the year. It never hurts to buy a book or two about business plans, to learn how they are set up and exactly the information that should be included in them. If you purchase a business plan software program, it's likely that there will be a guide included on the disk that will explain all of this stuff to you as well.

BRANDING YOURSELF

YOUR BRAND

You probably already know that branding is important to a business. It is important that a company be able to distinguish itself from the rest of the pack. When it comes to freelancing, it is about creating an identity that represents you. This may be in your style of writing, use of a logo or other mark or any other means off setting yourself apart from the many other freelancers out there. Your brand will work to give your potential clients their first impression of you and ultimately, it will serve to help you win new projects and build your business.

As a freelancer, while you may well use a recognizable mark or symbol so that potential clients will know you when they see it, the finished work that you do, or that is to say, your portfolio will serve as your real brand. Make no mistake about it for a minute: your brand and the overall impression that you give to your potential clients can be the deciding factor of whether you or your competitor gets the next project.

For the purposes of this book, it is assumed that the majority of your work will be found online, or through the mail, but there may likely come a time when you will have to meet a client face-to-face. Your appearance in that case can also serve as part of your brand. You must always put forth a professional appearance in the face of your clients, even if you spend the majority of your working hours in your underwear at home. If you decide to go further with your branding efforts, you can work on creating recognition for your name – this is done with logos and/or symbols. It can take years to build a successful brand, so don't believe for a minute that just because you choose a means that is unique from all the rest, that you will be instantly recognized. It took companies like McDonalds many years and millions and millions of dollars to gain the recognition that they now have.

WHAT CAN BRANDING DO FOR YOU?

Let's suppose that you and another freelancer are competing for the same job. As it happens in this example, you both have similar styles of writing and competence in the field in question. Your price is nearly double that which the other freelancer is charging. Part of the reason that you will win the job though your price is higher, is your brand. You are now beginning to be recognized because when clients see your brand, they know it has been around for awhile, and they see the quality.

Various materials that you present, such as your website define the level of service that you present to customers. A professional website presents to your clients that you act on a professional level and you are going to deliver a professional product.

If you have testimonials from other clients (and you should be working to get those all along), then you should be posting those on your website along with any awards you night have won along the way. So why will clients pay the higher price despite your work being very similar to the other freelancer's? PERCEPTION. Present yourself properly to you clients, and they will pay more every time.

Branding, when used correctly, will lead to more work, higher perceived value in your work and premium prices for your work.

That is the simple reason why branding for your business should be your top priority.

The best place to start with branding yourself is to consider what you stand for. How do you want your customers to view you? While you very well might be tempted to use every positive word you can think of to the list, you must try to focus on only two or three of these words. In short, the more clear and concise your message, the more powerful your brand will be. Consider the following as a few things that you might like your brand to stand for:

- Quality
- Experience
- Value
- Service
- Expertise
- Efficiency
- Reliability

Your ultimately goal is to own a word much the same way McDonald's owns "hamburger" or Volvo owns "safety. While the reality is that Volvo's are safety because they are well engineered, it's safety that people associate with the automobile. On a similar note, while a freelancer might be an expert in his or her field, and give excellent service, having clients to associate him or her with experience will likely have them trusting the freelancer with their important jobs.

So, to sum it up in a nutshell, while many consider branding to be nothing more than establishing a logo or service mark, it is actually much more. Your brand will always encompass one or more of the following, if not all of them:

- Visual
  - o Logo
  - o Color Scheme

- o Fonts
- o Signage
- o Promo Materials
- o Your Appearance
- Communications
  - o Tone of your written material
  - o Voicemail message
  - o Email style
  - o Level and speed of service
  - o Work process
  - o Invoice style, language and terms
  - o Contract
  - o Use of first, second or third person in copy
- Online appearance
  - o Email Signature
  - o Website usability
  - o Ways to contact you
  - o Your blog
  - o Your photo
  - o Your portfolio

In order to create an effective brand for yourself, you have to decide what it is that you want to represent. From there, you must express that value in everything that you do. The word that you have chosen will then form your core brand value. You understand of course that the most important part of the brand you are developing is YOU. Therefore, it is important that once you begin to establish your brand, you follow-through and live up to it at all times when it comes to business. Your personal disposition, appearance and personality must all reflect your brand when it comes to dealing with clients. On the other hand, many people choose to deal with a freelance writer because they do not want to deal with a larger company, so it's just as important that you do not feel that you have to present yourself as something you are not.

Once again, building a brand is not instant and it will take time. More likely than not, your brand is something that will develop as your career develops. The most important thing though, is that you decide on your core value from the very beginning so that when you begin to develop your brand image, they all work together in a unified image.

GIVING YOUR BUSINESS A NAME

The cornerstone of any brand is the brand name. As a freelancer, your brand name will be your business name. The following are qualities that you should look for in a name:

- Easy to spell
- Easy to pronounce
- Short and memorable
- Relevant domain name
- Reasonably unique name

Some freelance writers will choose to use their own name as their business. Others will not want to do that. There are some advantages and disadvantages either way:

- Personal Name
  - Advantages
    - Easy to come up with
    - Often a unique name
    - Descriptive
    - Often the easiest to find a domain for
    - Memorable
    - Usually easily Googled
  - Disadvantages
    - Not appropriate for expansion
    - Will not usually reflect your creativity
    - Will not reflect your brand values
- Non-Personal Name
  - Advantages
    - Free to find something catchy and fun
    - Can reinforce core brand values

- Can reference your services
- Can keep the name when you choose to expand
  - o Disadvantages
    - Harder to find a name that reflects your
    - Hard to find an appropriate domain name

Choosing to use a non-personal name can be worthwhile finding something that reflects your brand value. However, it's not essential as you can build brand value into a name. You can choose a made-up word for example, that literally means nothing, but over time, clients and the public in general will come to associate it with the service that you provide.

LOGOS, BUSINESS CARDS AND MARKETING MATERIALS

A substantial part of your brand is going to be the visual elements. The most important thing to remember when you develop your graphic identity is to think of every element as part of one core message. The logo you, choose, the colors, font choice and graphic elements should be consistent across all of the materials that you produce. They need to present themselves as if they come from the same family. The unity of expression presented forms a very professional image. Some of the materials you might apply include:

- Business cards
- Letterhead
- Email Signature
- Website
- Brochures
- Documentation like your invoices, quotes, estimates, etc

Consider the materials that other businesses use in their day-to-day operations. For example, why does Green Giant command a higher price than store brands? Do they taste better? In most cases, no, but the appearance that they present indicate that THEY ARE better. That's the same way it will work with your company. Maybe the writing is better or maybe it's not, but the appearance that you put forth can make all the difference in the world.

DESIGNING YOUR MATERIALS

There are multiple websites online today where you can purchase materials to create your unique designs for your logo and other business materials. The problem is that many others may also be purchasing these same images. However, if you have access to, and know your way around Photoshop, you can significantly change these images to make them your own.

Alternatively, you can hire a designer if your budget allows, who will design a completely unique image for you. Once the primary image is designed, it can be used to:

1. Create your website
2. Design Business Cards
3. Design other Marketing Materials
4. Design Forms like invoices, Statement, etc.

When you are looking for a designer, the first thing that you have to do is to work out an idea of what would best reflect your core value. As you search through the portfolio of each designer, look to see what they may have within it that matches a style that meets your needs.

Another thing that you can do is look through some print design books to find at least three examples of something that you are hoping to end up with and present that to the designer, who will come up with something unique that meets your needs.

BUDGET DESIGN SOLUTIONS

For some freelancers who are just starting out, hiring a professional designer is just not within the startup budget. If you fall into this category, do not despair. By using the following steps, you can come up with your own designs to use until you reach the point that a professional designer becomes more of an option for you:

1. Select your favorite font. Choose something simple. So-called "fancy" fonts are not always eye-pleasing to your clients, and in fact, some of them can be downright difficult to read.
2. Choose two or three colors that complement one another. Color palettes are easy to find. You can simply do a color search on Google for "color palette" and a number of options will appear for you. The color palette that you choose, should give you the hexadecimal numbers so that you can match them up in computer programs like Photoshop or something similar.
3. Write your business name out in your chosen font. Don't use multiple colors when writing your business name. If you business name is two or more words however, you may use one color for each word if you wish.
4. Choose a one or two color image for your logo. One color is actually better, but two is OK as well. When it comes to logos, the rule-of-thumb is the simpler it is, the better it will serve your purposes.
5. Now, use the business name as you have created it and the image you have chosen on all materials that you produce for your business including business cards, invoices, letterhead, etc.

YOUR BUSINESS WEBSITE

Your website is going to be the single most important tool at your disposal in your freelance writing business. The website is as important to branding your company as you are to completing the projects for your clients. The website is not only the first point at which potential new clients can learn more about you , but it is also where these potential clients cn have a look at your portfolio outside of business hours so that they can learn more about you. It is also a marketing tool in its own right and can perform many other functions as well if you have the right tools ands software available:

1. Securely deliver finished work through a download mechanism.
2. Provide multiple methods of contact such as an email form, your phone number, Skype info and more.
3. Take secure orders for work from clients.
4. Built-in payment mechanisms such as a secure gateway for clients to pay you.

You don't have to be a professional web designer to establish your online presence these days. There are literally thousands of website templates out there that can help you along the way. Simply customize them to your personal tastes and needs. There are also many free CMS (content management systems) programs on the internet such as Wordpress (http://www.wordpress.com) that you can upload and then manage from the admin section of the website. There are Wordpress templates available too that you can upload to your wordpress site and customize to suit your needs.

To find other CMS solutions of which many are free, though some are not, simply Google "content management". Some of these are so much in use, that there are a number of plugins and templates available, both free and paid, that help you to get the look and functionality that you want and need.

The website header should include your chosen logo image, and your business name the way it appears on your marketing materials. The domain name you choose should be the name of your business where possible. IN fact, you are a couple of steps ahead if you name your business based on a domain name that you like, that fits your business and chosen core values of your company.

The website should be aimed directly at your clients and potential clients. It's important to note that while your site should most definitely be professional, that doesn't mean that you have to have a cutting-edge website with all of the bells and whistles that a website can have these days. Your client is not interested in these things. They simply want to know that you are competent and professional, and can get their project done in a timely manner.

Your website should reflect YOU. Understand that when it comes to stock photography and other elements like that may have been seen hundreds of times by your clients, so use those sparingly. Instead, add your own photos and other such elements to the website to make it your own. Also, don't fill the website with marketing language that is vague, or even worse, with information that really doesn't fit what you do. Adding something simply for the sake of adding it because another site has it is the worse thing you can do.

Add testimonials to your site. You can get these in one of several different ways:

1. The client will automatically thank you
2. You can make use of surveys
3. You can write the client directly and ask them to give you a sentence or two of what they thought about your work. These are important and they go a long way into helping you to make a sale.

When you type the information about your company into the web pages, explain what you do in layman's terms. Don't use a lot of technical jargon tht will only serve to turn them off if they don't already know what you are talking about. Remember – clients are seeking you out because they want service on a personal level in most cases – not because you use some of the same type of language the big companies use.

Your call to action should be one that makes things as easy as possible for the client. Additionally, you should also give them as many ways of contacting you as possible. This includes email (form), phone, skype, Facebook, and any other way that you can think of. Add your phone number to the header image of your website as well. In fact, include ways to contact as often as it makes sense in your website. Repetition is key to helping your client to remember your contact information. The worst thing you can possibly do on your website is to tuck a link or your phone number away into some obscure corner of your website.

LET'S BUILD YOUR REPUTATION

Building your reputation can happens on three levels, but it takes work. It was once said by someone, that building a good reputation is hard work but gaining a terrible reputation is easy. Once you get something negative posted about you on the internet, it is extremely difficult to turn that around, so you must avoid it at all costs and instead, concentrate on doing things that will give potential clients an overall good view of you.

1. Building a reputation among your clients is the easiest way to build your reputation. All you have to do is consistently turn in good work, and you'll be theirs for life. In turn, having a good reputation with your clients will eventually lead to work indirectly from them, by way of gaining new clients when they tell others of your good work.
2. The next way to build your reputation is on the local level. Joining groups like your local Chamber of Commerce and other such organizations can lead to work from local companies.
3. Within the Industry is the other way you can build your reputation, when you start to become known as an expert in specific areas. This will eventually lead you to bigger and better projects that pay better. The most important thing, is that when you gain a reputation as an expert in specific fields, you gain respect from your clients which, in the end will lead to more work.

In many cases, you will not even have to be the best at what you do to become well-known in the industry. That's where reputation comes into play, and having a good relationship with your clients.

Now, with all that being said, building a good reputation depnds upon three different elements which include:

1. **You Must do Something to Set You Apart from Others** – The actions that you take to expand or improve upon your reputation depends entirely upon whether you want to focus on the industry as a whole, your clients or your local community.
   a. If your general focus is on your industry, you can perhaps consider speaking at a local event or something similar.
   b. If your focus happens to be the community at large, then perhaps you can speak at the Chamber of Commerce or some other similar group to target small business who may not know of your business at all, and perhaps so that they can gain more knowledge about your service and how you can help their company to grow.
   c. If you are concentrating on building your reputation among clients and potential clients, then perhaps you will want to concentrate on winning writing awards and other such programs. Again, producing consistently good work and providing amazing levels of customer service that people cannot help but to talk about will go a long way to building your reputation.
2. **You Must Generate Publicity** – Building a reputation is to become renowned in your industry. In order to accomplish that, you must be noticed. That means that you have to spend some time networking, attending various events and be seen at them, and volunteering for charitable activities such as fundraisers, etc.
3. Consistency is Key – There is a reason that a good reputation takes time to build. That is because there must be consistency over a period of time. You have to give clients time to realize just how special your business is, and once they do, they will begin to talk. You simply cannot give one client great service and then drop the ball with another and hope to maintain your reputation. Similarly, you can't write

just one article and expect to be called an expert in the field in question. It simply doesn't work that way and there isn't enough of your work available for judging to consider that you are an expert (yet).

While building a reputation is definitely difficult at times, the rewards available to be reaped are many. Along the way, you will gain respect and along with that, the respect and reputation will bring you better paying jobs.

In the next section of the book, we will take a look at what a typical workday should look like for you.

A TYPICAL WORKDAY

One of the benefits of having your own business is that you are now the master of your working destiny. Since you have full control of your day now, you can use the hours to do as you choose. On the other side of that, is the responsibility that comes along with it such as worrying about productivity, the company and what you can now do with your new found freedom.

Should You Have an Office in or out of the Home?

By now you should already know where your office is going to be. From an economical viewpoint, the home office is the obvious better choice. However, there are those who have the budget and wish to have an office outside the home. Whatever your choice, take another look at all of the options, and its potential benefits before you finalize your decision:

- **HOME** – There is something to be said about working from home. Just imagine – waking up, walking downstairs, still in your pajamas and you are at work! Home is actually where most freelance professionals get things up and running. As with anything, there are benefits and disadvantages to working from home.
  - o The Benefits Are:

- **SUPER CHEAP** – The biggest draw to freelancers who work at home is the fact that they don't have to worry about paying monthly rent for the space (other than your existing rent or mortgage). Add to that the fact that you can make use of existing phone and internet connections. In this case, you'll be able to recoup some, or most of the cost as business expenses when you file your taxes.
- **NO COMMUTE** – Commuting to and from work always takes up part of your day. This is generally time wasted and lost. If you are working at home you save money on fuel costs, possible tolls and wear/tear of your automobile. There's not even a worry about the time it takes to get ready for work, or whether you'll be late.
- **PEACE AND QUIET** – Depending on your current situation, working at home can provide you with more peace and quiet than you have ever experienced on the job. If there are children at home however, this can backfire on you.
- **PERSONAL ROUTINE** – When you work at home, you have the flexibility necessary to fit any important personal routines into your day. Whether you need time to exercise, make lunches for the family or just an afternoon nap, the choices is now all yours.
- **FREELANCERS WITH CHILDREN** – You can save a great deal of money on childcare expenses if you are working from home. It is understood that generally speaking, working hours at home are usually other than normal, so

- why not take advantage of that and fit your working hours around the rest of your schedule, which ultimately means that you can work whenever you want as long as you are meeting client deadlines and your work isn't suffering.
- **RELAXED AND CASUAL ATMOSPHERE** – Unless You have clients that visit you, you can literally work in your underwear.

o **DISADVANTAGES**
  - **DOESN'T LOOK PROFESSIONAL** – If you happen to be in an industry in which clients will have to come visit you, they may feel that your working from home is unprofessional in some cases, and perhaps that your company is unstable. On the other hand, many clients will realize that you are trying to cut costs, which in turn, typically means savings to them, so it may not be an issue at all. Additionally, if the setup of your home is such that there is a separate entrance, then this disadvantage is not so disadvantageous any longer.
  - **CLUTTERING UP THE HOUSE** – For some, there is more than enough clutter in the house without adding a bunch of office equipment. It depends on how you look at things, really. Again, if your office is one that has a separate entrance, then the two (home and office) can be easily separated.
  - **NO SEPARATION OF HOME/WORK** – If you can establish a set of rules for your family, and then adhere to them, this won't be much of a problem, but if you have small children at

home, and even some adult family members may fall into the category of constantly interrupting you. Many adults don't understand the concept of working from home, though that trend is changing, but it is extremely important that family understand that when you are in that office, YOU ARE WORKING! Otherwise, you'll never make your deadlines.

- **STRANGE HOURS** – It's already been mentioned earlier, but when you work from home, you may end up working some very strange hours, especially if it means completing a project before its deadline.
- **ALWAYS THE SAME** – Unless you are one where the errands keep you out of the house for a period of time each day, then it may seem like you never leave the house, and this can become very monotonous.

o **TIPS TO MAKE IT WORK**
   - **Have a Separate Space** – put your office in the spare room, or the basement, or some other place that forces you to walk from one end of the house to the other. If you have a garage, a section of that space can work perfectly as an office or study.
   - **Keep it near the front door** – if your business requires that you meet with clients in your office. Doing this prevents you from having to bring clients all through your home when they stop by.
   - **Get out of the house more** – If you do decide to setup a home office, set up certain time periods where you have to leave the house for a while. This is

especially true at "quitting time". You need to be able to unwind at the end of the day.

OFFICE SPACE RENTAL

Renting a small office near your home, perhaps even close enough to walk can curb the problem of feeling like you are stuck in the house all the time. If your budget allows for it, go for it! For some reason, many freelancers find it to be very satisfying when they know they have their own office to go to. At the time of this writing, I am planning on actually moving into an RV full-time. I plan to hit the road in September 2016, leaving Maryland and heading to California, giving up the so-called brick and mortar life for one where I can be in California one day, and perhaps Nevada or Arizona the next. Personally, I am a nomad at heart, and with technology such as it is, there's no reason for me not to, then I can plan on meeting clients at THEIR OFFICES instead of them coming to mine.

All that being said, there are a number of advantages to having an actual office to go to and they include:

- **PROFESSIONAL LOOK AND FEEL** – While working from your home can appear unprofessional to some of your clients, having an actual office to go to will definitely be professional to all of them.
- **SEPARATES WORK AND HOME** – There is a definite distinction between being home and being at work. As a business owner, you will still find yourself taking work home on occasion to meet a deadline, but then again, in the large businesses, this happens a lot as well.
- **FORCES YOU TO TURN OFF THE SWITCH** – having to go home forces you to call it a day at some point and go home to rest. Whether you walk or drive, it

gives you time to unwind a little

Then of course, there are the disadvantages to having office space, just like there are disadvantages to anything else. These disadvantages include, but are in no way limited to any or all of the following:

- **EXPENSIVE** – Office space adds additional bills including rent, utilities, and perhaps other costs in certain situations.
- **OLD MEMORIES** – Many freelancers enjoy the freedom of having escaped the office when they decide to start a freelance writing business. If you are one of these, then try working from home for a while before actually opening your own office.
- **YOU ARE COMMUTING AGAIN** – If the office you decide to rent is not very close to your home, then you are right back to commuting again, which was likely one of the reasons you wanted to start a freelance writing company to begin with.

TIPS

- **START SMALL** – When you are looking for an office space, you might be tempted to go all out and get a huge space, with the latest styles in furniture for the office. DON'T. As a startup, your office need only be a room large enough to hold the furniture and equipment that you need to get started. The fancy stuff can come later after you have successfully established yourself in the industry. If you spend a lot of money, and for some reason things do not work out, you're going to have all this expensive furniture that is only going to serve as a reminder of the money spent to acquire it. As you grow your business, and your budget allows, a larger space and better furnishings can be purchased without breaking the budget or putting it into a deficit.

- **GET SOMEWHERE NICE AND LIGHT** – Renting cheap offices can be like renting a jail cell. While staying inside of the budget, see if you can find a location with at least one window.
- **GET A PLACE NEARBY** – Most areas of the city in which you live will have areas already built and configured for office space, so try to avoid aiming for the heart of your city for office space. Find a location as close as possible to your house so that you can avoid, or even eliminate any commute.

WORKING ELSEWHERE

From first glance, it seems that our only choices of workspace is from home or from a rented office space. That's not true however. There are several alternatives including the public library, which is a good option due to the quiet atmosphere. They usually have all of the amenities you will need. The one downside though, is the internet connection. If your public library is one that is very busy, the Wi-Fi they provide may seem like the old dial-up internet of days gone by. Still, when you consider that you will have no rent to pay, utilities to worry about, or an internet bill even, then perhaps the slow Wi-Fi will be a non-issue for you.

Other options include local coffee shops, or even working outdoors. Even McDonald's offers free Wi-Fi these days, though it's probably not possible to spend the entire day there, but the point is that there are many other options other than working directly from home if that is something that you do not want to do.

MAKE YOUR WORKSPACE A HAPPY PLACE

Having your own business is going to be a drag if it's dreary and dark. Taking the time to properly set up your office and to brighten it are extremely important. My workspace is a room in my house that has a sofa, desk, filing cabinet, several different printers and other office type equipment. I get into fits where I absolutely have to sit at the desk so I can work. At other times, I prefer to sit on the sofa, with the television playing as I write. For most people, the television will perhaps be a distraction, but for me, at times, it is my muse. If I am writing under one of my pen names (I have several), then I will have a movie on that is somehow related to what I am writing. For instance, when I am writing about serial killers then I will have some sort of murder movie on television.

On the other hand, when I am writing a how-to book such as this one, I have AC/DC playing in the background. The point is that you have to make your workspace a place that you enjoy being so that you do not feel like you are doing something that you hate.

WORKING ERGONOMICALLY

It doesn't matter whether you work from home or an office, you have to work ergonomically. There are several ways to setup your office so that is both a productive workspace and a healthy one. The ideal workspace will minimize your risk of injury and it will also make it easier for you to stay organized. Consider the following:

- **YOUR LOCATION** – Your desk would ideally face the door of the office. Studies have shown that this is the most calming position for the desk to be for the occupant of the office. It is also known to be the most welcoming position for someone who is entering the room.
- **NATURAL LIGHT** – Where possible, your office should include plenty of natural light. Having a window in the also gives your eyes a break from the work, allowing you to look out periodically without losing track of time.
- **YOUR CHAIR** – Your chair, in all likelihood, will be the space that you will occupy for at least eight hours of your day, if not more. To this end, it's well worth the cost of investing in a very good one. When making your purchase, make use of display models and sit in them to see if it is a good fit for you.

- **YOUR DESK** – Your desk obviously has to be one that you are comfortable sitting at. A student desk, for example, is functional, but it's not very big and you will be out of workspace before you even sit down to work. The desk has to have plenty of space for you to work from, and it has to be the proper height.

- **COMPUTER SCREEN** – As a general rule of thumb, your screen should never be brighter than the brightest point in the room. This means, NEVER WORK IN A DARK ROOM! Glare and reflections on your computer screen are distracting and it is also bad for your eyes. You should always avoid facing your computer screen towards a light source and finally, your computer screen should always be at least an arm's length away from you. When you are sitting, your computer screen should be positioned so that you are staring straight ahead and that your neck is relaxed.

- **YOUR KEYBOARD** – The computer keyboard should be close to the computer screen. This way, when you are typing, your elbows are relaxed and resting on the desk. It also reduces the strain on your wrists.

TIPS AND TRICKS FOR THE WORKSPACE

- **LOCK THE DOOR** – You'll never get anything done with kids and household pets running throughout the room when you are trying to work. The best thing you can do in the case of kids being at home while you are supposed to be working is to make them understand that just because you are home, you are still working. Explain to them that when the door is locked, you are not to be disturbed unless it is a true emergency. It may seem harsh at first, but if you truly intend to make this business venture work, then you will have to set parameters and then stick to the rules. If you deviate from the rules, then they will not take you seriously and they will deviate on a regular basis, setting up the failure of your new venture.

- **BRIGHT LIGHT** – If your workspace feels like it is dark, turn on more lights, get brighter bulbs, open window blinds, or whatever else it takes. If you have done all of that, add a couple of mirrors to the walls. These will reflect the light, and if they are large enough, they will even make the room seem larger.
- **REMOVE ALL CLUTTER** – You will be spending a great deal of time in this room. It's worth it to keep the room clutter-free. You'll be happier with a clean office, and your productivity will show-through. Anything that is not related to your business should be gone from the room
- **GET RID OF DARK WALLS** – If the color of the room is dark, or it has patterned wallpaper, consider changing them to white. White helps to reflect the light in the room, making it brighter, and it will also serve to keep you alert.
- **WHITE BOARD** – A white board or bulletin board will help you to stay organized. Get into the habit of posting important notes on it, and checking it regularly will keep you reminded of important tasks that need completed, plus it will get you out of the chair once in a while.

EQUIPMENT YOU WILL NEED

- **COMPUTER** – This is a necessity. Most households have at least one. If there is only one computer in the house and everyone uses it, then you will need to probably consider buying one specifically for your business. There's nothing worse than going to the family computer to finish a project for a client only to find out it was messed up by one of the children or something similar.
- **PRINTER** – As a writer, it really will not matter what type of printer you use, but different printers are handy for different projects. A laser printer is more economical

than an ink jet, so I use one for black and white printing. I also have a color inkjet printer that I use to print invoices, and anything else that I use a touch of color in.

- **FAX MACHINE** – As it happens, a stand-alone fax machine is really outdated these days. All you really need is a multi-function machine, or at least a scanner, then you can fax over the internet using one of the many services available. For my office, my laser printer is a Brother, and my color printer/scanner combination is a Canon. I use the Canon to scan whatever I need to fax, and then I use an online service to fax whatever needs faxed.

BACKUP, BACKUP, BACKUP!!!

I can't stress how very extremely important this is. You cannot even imagine how many important projects have been lost for reasons starting with the kids messed them up to the hard drive crashing, and yes, that happens a lot. Over the last 15 years, I have had three catastrophic failures of my hard drive. The first one was all it took for me to learn to backup.

I now backup everything, everyday. The same thing goes with antivirus software. Make sure you use it. It will save your business life many times over. I work from a laptop. I also keep a second laptop on hand in case of problems with my main computer.

As you grow your business, you are going to want to consider backing up your material over the internet and to a server. This gets all important material into a location away from your office in case a catastrophic event happens which can be any number of things such as theft of your equipment, or God-forbid, a fire.

You're also going to want to buy a surge protector. While much stronger than they once were, a computer and its ancillary equipment is something that will not stand a power surge. Power surges come when lightning hits the house and from other sources as well. A surge protector will prevent this from ruining your equipment.

AVOIDING REPETITIVE STRAIN INJURIES

Repetitive strain injury consists of several conditions that crop up as a result of overuse of the computer and includes Carpal-Tunnel Syndrome among other things. Freelancers are especially at high-risk for such injuries because they work in unconventional setup, they work late at night, or for very long hours, working alone because we have no natural interruption of the work-flow.

As a freelancer you have to be aware of these types of injuries and work toward avoiding any of the causes. Remember – you no longer have sick days to take when you are affected by them. If the injuries get bad, there is a chance it could seriously hamper your freelance career, not to imagine the fact that you will be absolutely miserable.

Some of the warning signs that these types are setting in include pain in the upper body, including the neck, shoulders, upper back, wrists, hands or fingers.

You might also have tingling or numbness, as though the affected area has lost circulation. You might also have weakness or fatigue in the affected areas.

YOUR POSTURE IS IMPORTANT

We all remember our teachers telling us to sit up straight. Perhaps mom or grandma said the same things to us. It was actually all for our own good, though we probably felt that it was just another thing for them to pick on us about.

The truth of the matter is that good posture is extremely important in your work space. It starts with you having your chair set at the proper height. You have to push your hips back into the seat as far as they will go. It will feel weird to your at first in most cases. This is because we spend much of our lives sitting with the incorrect posture. When sitting, your feet should be flat on the floor, and the adjustment height of the chair should have your knees at the same level as your hips.

If the armrests are adjustable on your chair, adjust them so that you are able to relax in the chair with the arms on the armrests. If you have to sit with your shoulders hunched, you're going to be uncomfortable, and end up with one of the injuries mentioned earlier. If the armrests cannot help you to sit in a relaxed manner, then you should remove them from the chair. The chair should be adjusted so that it is exactly straight up and not leaning back. Your entire back, when you are sitting in other words, should be straight.

Take breaks regularly. There are a great many freelancers who sit for hours without ever moving. Your body was not designed to do this. You have to get up periodically and move around.

Every half-hour or so, take a little break, even if it's for only two or three minutes. Stretch your body, and then sit back down to work. Perhaps even walk around for five or ten minutes. Place objects further away than arms-length so that you have to reach to get them.

Don't eat at your desk. Get up from the desk and go to your kitchen if your office is at home to have your lunch. If you are in an office that you rented, move to another part of the room to have lunch.

U can keep your office environmentally friendly even thought you use a lot of electric equipment. Turn your computer off at the end of the day to save on electricity. You can make recycling easy by placing paper in one receptacle, bottles and cans in another, and plastics in still another.

For documents that stay in house, or that you print simply for proofing, use both sides of the paper. When you write letters to clients that you will mail, use both sides of the paper then as well.

Buying recycled paper also helps the environment as well. When you end up with empty ink and laser cartridges, don't put them in the trash. Take them to a location that specializes in recycling them. Many places will provide you with free mailers to send the cartridges back to them.

Don't print emails and other such documentation unless you really have to. Read them from the computer screen. Using natural light from outside wherever possible is not only helpful to your eyes, but it will save on electricity as well. Finally, use email instead of snail mail wherever possible to save on paper and ink.

Above all else, make sure that you STAY PRODUCTIVE. As a freelancer, it's easy to lose focus. Especially if we are working on a project that we feel is boring. Staying organized will help you to stay focused on the task at hand.

Use To-Do lists to stay in focus of what you have to get done. If you do not complete the list that work day, move the things that are not yet done to the next day's list. To-Do lists can be made for the entire week or even month, in advance, giving you an idea of what's on the agenda ahead of time.

While it was previously mentioned that any incomplete tasks should be put on the next day's list, keep in mind that what is actually happening is you are getting backed up, which means possibly working later in the day to get things finished, or even working on the weekends, which kind of goes against why you wanted to strike out on your own to begin with. So, the bottom line, is to stay focused on your work so that you don't get behind. On the other hand, don't make the list so long that you'll never complete it to begin with.

Keep track of your time. This is required if you are billing by the hour, but it is still useful in running your business. When you track the time you spend on a project, even one that you are billing a flat-rate for, it will give you an idea of how much time you actually spent on that project, so you can adjust bids accordingly on your next job that is similar. Time tracking will let you know in other words, whether or not you are actually making a reasonable wage from your projects, with enough room to still turn a profit for the company.

DISTRACTIONS

If you haven't yet thought about it, you will now. Working in an office for a boss is much, much different than working for yourself. You could in some ways compare it to transitioning from high school to college. In high school, the teacher took attendance and if you missed you were queried as to why you missed, etc. In college, you either show up, or you don't. Your grades will dictate whether or not you receive credit for the class. If you miss days in college, where there was no work requirement, or the instructor allowed you to make missed work up, then no big deal. It happens. You will be tempted to slack off.

As an employee of another, you will get the same pay whether or not you work hard. The end result however, is that you may ultimately get fired or miss out on being promoted. It's a fact of life, and deep in your mind you know this, so the tendency is to work harder so that you don't lose your job.

When you're working for yourself, you're going to think "I'm my own boss, so I don't have to push as hard." That's not true though. Sure, you won't get into trouble. You are, after all, the boss, but if you miss deadlines, that client may well leave you. In short, if you are not working, you are not making money, and any idle time, is wasted time. It's important that you establish a good work ethic early in your business.

Always start the day on the right foot. Many freelancers will wake whenever they want, and work through for eight hours or more, and that seems fine, they're working, right? Well, it's basically a recipe for disaster. Consider your client-base. What hours are they normally working? Stopping work for another company and striking out on your own was one of the reasons that you quit your day job. Right? Remember you wanted to be able to deal with your clients during their regular working schedule? If you establish your business hours from noon to 9:00 p.m., then that's fine, but if you establish your working hours as 8:00 a.m. until 5:00 p.m. and you're not starting until noon, you've done lost half of the day. Establish a morning routine, and then stick with that routine.

Many freelancer's will procrastinate on a project until the last minute. I was once guilty of doing that as well, but it is a recipe for disaster. Make your own deadline perhaps, two or three days prior to the client's deadline, and then you will have time to look over the work you did and fix any problems that you find.

The best thing you can do, is to establish regular business hours, and then stick to them. It's a necessary evil that there will be times that you will have to work late. In many cases, it's unavoidable, but if you establish a regular schedule and stick to it, you will find that you are getting your work done well-ahead of time, which ultimately leaves you more time to find more work.

During times when you have no projects to work on, and there will be those times too, then you need to be reading materials related to your industry. Things change fast, and your client's needs will change too. For instance, perhaps your client is accustomed to having his or her projects completed in a certain manner. As it happens, this clients website depends on content to ultimately generate income for their company. Well, you happen to know that Google changed its algorithm once again, and that the way your client currently does business and has the content rendered is now a method that Google will penalize. You can advise your client of these changes ahead of time so that they can change the way they have things done, ultimately saving them money in the end. You have now gained another level of respect from that client because you have helped them in their business model.

You should also attend industry events on a regular basis, even if it means working late to complete current projects. These events help you meet more people, who could potentially bring you more business and they also help to keep you on top of new additions or changes to industry practices.

Another way to stay on top of things is to subscribe to any and all industry related magazines and newsletters that you can. They are all great learning tools, and while one newsletter or magazine may seem the same as another, the truth is that if you find even one small blurb that is different, it is well-worth having read the issue for that one small bit of information.

Networking with others in your line of work is also important to staying on top of things. Facebook and even Twitter are great for not only staying in touch with your colleagues but also picking up new and interesting bits of information.

In short, any thing that you can do to keep up with changes, new information, etc. is important and must be made part of your day.

FIGHTING LONELINESS

It sounds strange, but while you may at the beginning relish the idea of working alone, the truth is that at some point in time, you will begin to feel lonely in your work. Here are some ways to fight that loneliness:

1. Meet with, or at least call clients regularly.
2. Attend industry events
3. Take a daily walk at or around lunch time.
4. Take your laptop work in a coffee shop or at the library for a while. The library is also a great place to be when you are researching a project for a fresh perspective over what is available to you on the internet.

For everything that is going on, whether it something positive or negative, you can take steps to make things to work in your favor.

FINDING YOUR CLIENTS

The hardest part of your entire business is going to be finding clients. There are some brokerages out there that will help you to get started. Some of them however, retain the clients as their clients, and you never know who you are really dealing with, and when the client returns for more work, they are free to choose you, or not.

That's fine to start out, but what you really want to do is to search for clients that are yours, with no middle-man taking fees. Virtually every business in the world, including many so-called "mom and pop" shops now have websites. In order to bring people to those websites through organic search, they are going to need CONTENT. Businesses of course need writing done for a variety of other reasons as well. Start locally and advertise your services, but, let's take a step back first to see what you are going to need when a client DOES answer your advertising.

PORTFOLIO

One of the first things a client is going to wonder about when you are wooing them for their business, is whether or not you can actually write. A portfolio answers this question for them. You can build a portfolio within your own website, but that involves buying yet more software. You can use one of the many available sites online to display your portfolio as well, and then when business starts to grow, you can purchase the necessary software to host the portfolio yourself, if you choose.

If your website is one that is professional, you've got half the battle won already. You can post links on one of your web pages to material that you have already published online. For materials not published online for whatever reason, you can use one of the aforementioned portfolio sites. Make sure they are professionally written, edited and spell-checked. There's nothing worse than trying to land a client and the samples they are looking at are fraught with mistakes.

Choose the work that you want to display publicly, very carefully. Work that is less than stellar should be omitted from the list you provide. On the outset, you will have very little work to show anyone, much less to have a full and bursting portfolio. There will be a number of reasons for this. In a case of work for hire, the client may forbid you to show the work you completed for them, because they are passing it off as their own. This is perfectly acceptable in the online world. So what do you do when you have very little to present to a client?

In such a case, what you should do is write some articles for no other purpose than to bulk up the portfolio. You can also search out some charities that need work done, and those articles could perhaps be tax deductible (you'll have to consult your account to be sure) but in any case, it can help to grow the portfolio.

YOUR FIRST LEADS

Clients are going to be difficult to come by when you first start out as I already said. Starting with places locally is your best bet to find those initial projects. Agencies like the local Chamber of Commerce and other business associations can be helpful. If you are a traveling writer, like I will soon be doing, then that may not be a viable option.

Looking online at some of the broker sites like Zerys.com will provide you with some work, but the clients are never yours. In fact, with most of these sites, you are not allowed to share contact information to preserve the integrity of the sites, but still, it's a source of income as you seek out your own clients.

Friends and family can be helpful as well. While they will not usually have work for you, unless of course they own or run a business, but they will generally be happy to pass around business cards to people that they know who may need your services.

Make sure to let people know that you are looking for work. If you don't tell anyone, then they can't hire you, nor can they pass the word around that you are a freelance writer. Consider emailing any friends or family that you think might be willing to help, plus you can post on the social networks like Facebook that you are available. Former (or current) co-workers can also be helpful. Don't be afraid to let people know. You are after all, in business now!

Remember the old saying that "beggars cannot be choosers". Take any work that comes along, whether it pays your rate or not. $5.00 for a 500 word article is much better than zero dollars for the wasted time not working. Remember that those low-paying jobs will often lead to higher paying jobs. It's also another notch in your portfolio as well, in most cases. As you begin to build your portfolio, then you can work in price increases.

ADVERTISING FOR WORK

You'll read more about this later, but advertising using services like Google Adwords, and buying ad space on related websites can find you some clients. Your marketing materials should ALWAYS give all your contact information so that potential clients know how to get in touch with you.

When you complete a project for a client, be sure to let them know that you are available for their next project as well. Always work hard to stay in the good graces of your clients. Work on them referring other clients to you as well. Make sure your business is "referable". You are referable when you complete quality work, offer fabulous customer assistance, complete work on time, etc.

If your work is borderline, or even not so good, you will not be referable and business will suffer. When a customer refers another business to you, you must be on top of your game, or it will not only make you look bad, but the referring client will be leery of sending anyone else to you as well.

Everything that you do must focus on winning the "game" of business. When clients refer winners to their colleagues, it makes them look good too, so if you are churning out fantastic work, the client who referred the colleague to you looks good, and they are likely to refer even more business to you. You always want to deliver quality work, on time, every time. Don't let up, even for a minute on the quality that you deliver.

Reliability is an absolute must. If you make a promise to a client, be sure that you are going to be able to follow-through. Promising something to a client simply because you think that is what they want to hear is a recipe for disaster.

Always make sure your prices are in line with the service you are offering. If you charge top dollar, then the client should be getting top of the line work. When you are starting out, no one knows you yet, so you might have to start with prices a little lower than what you feel your work is worth. That's OK. It's to be expected. You can always gradually increase your prices as time goes on.

Finally, always be friendly. You can have top notch, quality work and reasonable prices, but if you have a bad attitude, or the client perceives you as being abrasive, they will stop dealing with you. Only give clients reason to like you, not the other way around.

Other things that you can do to gain work are relatively simple, but go a long way in making you look like a professional. One of them is to give your clients a personal guarantee. You should only start using something like this when you are experienced though. When you are just starting out, you will find yourself spending a lot of time fixing things instead of creating new work. Offering a money –back promise can be helpful in landing you that next project, but frankly, you may want to keep a close eye on it when you do. If you find you are refunding money to particular clients, then they may be simply taking advantage of you. Most clients will not ask for their money back, but there are those who will every chance they get. This type of person is rare, but they are around. Be vigilant in seeking out those who are simply trying to get free work out of you.

Give great customer service. I say this a lot, but the truth is, a customer who is getting great customer service is one who will be willing to pay a premium for it.

Always offer free consultations. You will reap the rewards in the end instead of trying to bill a client an hourly rate to help them with their needs. When a customer likes you, and you are giving them what they need by way of great work, great customer service, etc., they will be receptive to you when they are asked to refer other work to you. Always make it easy for them to refer other work to you, and then ask them to do it.

Offering incentives can help to increase the referral work load as well. Do it tastefully though. You don't want the client to get the impression that you are trying to buy them off.

Consider establishing an affiliate program on your website. Affiliate programs are outside the context of this book, but basically, you offer a payment of a fixed amount to people who refer clients to you. There is a number of different ways you can do this. You can offer a percentage of the total amount spent by the referred client, or you can offer a fixed amount for each person that they refer, whether the person buys or not. Be careful with that one though, and make sure the software is able to differentiate IP addresses so that a crooked person cannot send the same person repeatedly to you, jacking up the fees that you owe them.

Sometimes asking clients to refer other clients to you can be difficult, or even somewhat embarrassing, but fear not – there's nothing wrong with seeking out more work, as long as it does not interfere with the business relationship between you and the person you are asking to refer others to you.

MEETING WITH POTENTIAL NEW CLIENTS

You'll get a few projects right away just by virtue of the fact that they contacted you. In most case however, when a client contacts you, you simply have your foot in the door. The good news is that half of the battle is won. On the other hand, you will still have to woo them with your abilities. Meeting with new clients is like going to a job interview. Nearly everyone gets nervous during these meetings. There are some things that you can do to make your meetings go easier.

1. **Always be yourself** – The client knows you are a freelance writer. While you don't necessarily have to dress to the nines, it's probably not a good idea to show up in a t-shirt, cutoff shorts and flip-flops. It's not necessary to pretend to be a larger company than you are. They will see right through that, and besides, they

are likely looking to work with a smaller company anyway so that they can get the personal attention to their projects that they are looking for.

2. **Be prepared** – The best way to work around your stress is to prepare well for your meeting. Have your portfolio and anything else that you want to present ready.

3. **Know what you want to say beforehand** – Make note cards so that you don't forget anything. Make sure to outline any strengths that you bring to the table. By knowing what you want to say, and what you may want to ask the client ahead of time, you will find that your stress over the meeting was unwarranted.

4. **Be on time** – nothing looks worse for you and your company, than to show up late for a meeting. If you are late for the meeting, the client will be left with the impression that your delivery of their important projects is going to be late as well.

5. **Don't be afraid to say no** – You probably already know that every project is not going to be right for you. When a client presents a project to you, make sure that you are going to be able to meet the criteria they require and that you will be able to deliver on time. It's far better to turn down a project if you have doubts, than it is to gain a reputation for not delivering as promised.

6. **Don't quote prices on the spot** – There are too many variables. Giving a quote may be easy if the project is something that you might happen to know, but if research is involved, then there are certain things you are going to have to take into consideration before you quote a price.

7. **Ask questions** – you need to know every detail about the project before you conclude the meeting with the client. Ascertain exactly what the client expects. At the conclusion of the meeting, go back to your office and take a long look at the project, estimate how long the research will take, and then the actual writing of the project, then, and only then, you can email a quote to the client for them to either approve or decline.

8. **No free samples** – Your portfolio contains (or should) everything a client needs to see in order that they make a decision as to whether or not to hire you. If a client asks you to write a piece free of charge, as a sample of your work, politely decline. Most clients who are serious about hiring you will not even ask, but there are a few who will get you to write a sample piece that they will use, and then move on to the next freelancer to try and do the

same. This sounds ridiculous I know, but there are people out there that do this.

Financial security is a big deal for freelancers. Always make sure that you have some cash reserves to carry you through the lean times. While you are doing the occasional project for a client, be sure to keep your eyes peeled for projects that are ongoing, such as weekly blog posts, etc. While we all dream of the big projects that will pay the bills for a couple of weeks or even a month or more, the reality is that the little projects will help to carry you through. Still, a weekly blog post with a $20.00 price attached to it means that you will get that every week. Get a handful of those, and you will quickly get to where you want to be.

You also want to be on the lookout for opportunities to earn passive income. Passive income is where you do a project once, but it keeps paying you. This can mean writing an article for your own blog, and then placing an affiliate ad on the page that is related to that article. It can also mean writing an article for a company in which they pay you to produce it, and then pay you royalties for so many page views, etc.

Make sure that you pace yourself. You'll be tempted to take every project that comes your way, and you can if you plan correctly, but never take on so much work that you start missing deadlines. Make sure that each project you take can be completed after finishing your current project and so on. By all means, work on filling your calendar with every project you can get, but when you find that too many things are going to come due at the same time, make sure you can actually deliver it within that time without angering a client because their project came in after it was due.

Remember, especially when dealing with major publications, that their editorial calendars stay the same, regardless of whether you have one or ten projects. You delivering their project late is going to screw up their production calendar and may well lose you a valuable client. Also, remember that each client, regardless of how much they spend with you, is a valuable client.

When starting out, push yourself a little to see where your limits are. You can always back off, but it will give you a good idea of your productivity when work is coming in fast and hard.

MARKETING YOUR TRADE

The first thing you need to do when you begin to market your services is to define your target market. You may say "Everyone is a potential client" but that's not true. There is a specific sector that you are going to want to target and that's what we need to figure out here.

There are several key points you need to nail down before you can point a finger at your target market. The first is to choose whether you wish to work with big companies or small businesses. While you may very well end up with work from both at one time or another, your marketing efforts must focus on one. From there you need to decide which industry you want to work within. Again, while you may end up with work in a number of niches, you are going to want to focus on one, perhaps two so that you can specialize in those areas. For example, say you focus on writing about dogs as your primary niche expertise. Then it's unlikely you are going to know a great deal about medical procedures without doing some significant research. At some point you may get hired to write some sort of medical article, but your niche is going to be dogs, and perhaps cats.

That example was simply to illustrate the differences the client will see. You can make your choices on just about anything you want. Maybe you're not an expert now in a niche that you want to work in, but that will come with time. That said, perhaps you want to work in a niche that pays particularly well. Perhaps you know of a niche where the pay may not be as high as it is in some industries, but is underserved with plenty of work to be had. The choices are all yours, but once you choose, you need to work hard at becoming good at what you do, so that in the end, clients will be seeking you out instead of you looking for them.

There are independent writers out there, right now, who make six figure salaries, and have so much work that they turn work away. With hard work and diligence, you can obtain that status too. The whole idea is that you focus on one or two areas, and start from there. If you know someone that works in a particular industry, then you may already have a foot in the door and you just don't realize it yet.

AIM YOUR PITCH

Now that you know who your target market is, you need to work on how to best present yourself and your services to that market. Here are some suggestions on how you can present yourself to your potential clients, telling them about your services:

1. **Target your portfolio to your client list**. If you are trying to target large companies, you're going to want to emphasize any experience you have in that industry. Less is more in many cases. Your portfolio should leave out, in other words, anything not related to the potential client's business.
2. **Tailor your pitch** – Whatever method you are using to pitch yourself to your client, you need to tailor your pitch to that specific client and their needs. You need to be saying the right things to each individual client, short of making exaggerations, in order to win their business.
3. **Fit the way you dress and speak to the situation** – The way you dress and speak makes a huge difference in business deals. As a general rule of thumb, emulate what the

business does. If they are dressed casually, then you should as well. If they are in suits, then you should be as well.

I mentioned previously about building a reputation. The reputation that you build will play a huge part in how you position yourself within your market. Just like a celebrity, there is a chance you will be stereotyped and known specifically for doing a certain type of work. That's not always a bad thing, but there will come a time where things may get stagnate in one area. It's important that while you present to a client that you are the perfect fit for their company, you also show that you can be versatile and do nearly anything.

THE MARKETING CYCLE

At its best, it can be difficult to determine exactly which marketing strategies yield the best results. The marketing cycle consists of several parts that can help you to determine what is working best for you. Basically it breaks down into three different parts including planning, activity and review.

PLANNING STAGE

On your computer, open a page on Microsoft Word or whatever word processing program you use and define four different categories on the page including:

1. **Target Market** – Who is the target market you wish to focus on? Spend some time to research this aspect of the marketing plan, if you have not already done so. Once you figure out the market you wish to target, you will need to define the best media with which to reach them. What are your competitors doing to reach them?
2. **Plan of Action** – How can you reach your target market? Consider the contacts that you might have. Also consider what strategy might best appeal to your target market. A little later on, we'll give you some ideas on that aspect.

3. **Timeframe** – What is the estimated time in which you will execute each of the strategies you have chosen?
4. **Marketing Goals** – Identify goals in the marketing plan that you can measure. While you already know that the goal is to find work, it is vital that you define specific goals that are measurable. For instance, a measurable goal could be: "Contact at least five leads". A non-specific goal might be to "get more work". When you start out, plan only a few measurable goals so that you are able to track them back to the strategy that worked.

ACTION STAGE

Once you have planned your goals, then it's time to act upon those goals. You should also plan to spend some time each week with your marketing plan. You will always believe that client time is more important, but you really need to check your plan occasionally to update it and measure the performance of your goals.

REVIEW STAGE

This touches on the action part of the plan as well. It is extremely important that some time be set aside regularly to review the plan and examine the lessons that you learned. Did your goals work out? Did you obtain more clients? Using the knowledge you gained, revise the marketing plan and eliminate goals that did not work, and increase the expectations of those that did work out.

It's entirely up to you to determine the cycle's length for each update of the marketing plan. If you have a heavy workload, then perhaps you want to make your cycles three or six months long. Whatever timeframe you choose, you must be consistent in working to meet your goals.

As a freelancer, you should always be prepared to promote your business, whatever situation you might find yourself in. You never know when you might run into someone who could use your services. It's good to be prepared with some marketing materials, and at the very least, some business cards to pass around to potential clients.

A business card is an essential and probably the most used tool in your arsenal. When you purchase cards, you should make sure that they are legible and easy to read. Be sure that you include all avenues of contact. Make sure to make it as easy as possible for a client to contact you. For myself, as a traveling writer, I have settled on providing a cell phone contact, email conact and I let potential clients know directly on the cards that they can use the contact form on my website.

Your business cards should be professionally designed and of the standard size so that they will fit easily into a business card holder. Keep them crisp and pristine. It looks bad when you hand a crumpled business card to a potentially new client.

If you attend industry events, it's common practice, and in fact, expected that you will hand out business cards during the event. Also be prepared to hand out cards during networking events. Even if a potential client forgets about the card, they will be reminded of you when they find it in their pocket later on down the line.

When we speak to others, it's human nature to speak humbly about what it is we do. BREAK THAT HABIT OF BEING HUMBLE. Always try to be selling yourself when you speak to people about your business and what you do. In some cases, speaking of your business can be inappropriate, but the fact is that nearly everyone will be interested in hearing what it is that you do.

Many times, when you meet new people, they will ask what it is that you do – don't be afraid to tell them, nor to show your excitement for the work you do.

I'm sure you have heard it said many time that it's not what you know, but who you know. THIS IS TRUE. Simply put, the more people that know you and know what it is that you do, the more people who will be in some sort of position to refer work to you. We've all been in a conversation at one time or another, in which a person says that they need this particular thing done, and the other guy says "I know a guy…"

A good impression will almost ensure that when the time for a referral pops up, it will be you that the person names rather than someone else. All that being said, it's really a good idea to show up at industry events, if for no other reason than to simply network with others and pass around business cards and/or other marketing materials.

Marketing yourself in person is only one way to get yourself out there to potential clients. There are a number of other ways that you can market your services to your target market. We list a few of them here, but you should invest in a book that is specifically geared toward marketing ideas and can help to take you to the next level in your marketing plan.

1. **Word of Mouth** – producing good work and having happy clients will slowly start to create a buzz about your services. It takes time, but as long as you are consistent, people within the industry will begin to talk. You can jump start the process a little however by utilizing the contacts within your network of people such as:
   a. Have family and friends who work within the industry to tell others about you.
   b. Send emails to all of those in your address book telling them what you now do.
   c. Ask satisfied clients to refer new work to you.
   d. Offer free consultations to new referrals.
   e. Consider a referral program (affiliate program) that will compensate those who send potential clients to you.
2. **Clients** – More likely than not, your client will need many projects completed as opposed to a one off job. Delivering quality work and great customer service will nearly always bring that extra work your way. Follow these steps to get

more work from clients:

    a. Contact clients you have not worked for in a while and ask them if they have anything that they need to have done.

    b. Contact everyone on your client list when you begin offering new services to let them know. This will also serve to remind them that you are there for their next writing project.

    c. Start a newsletter to send out to your client base. This will also serve to notify them of new develops at your company. Remember though to remove them from your mailing list if they ask.

    d. Use your email signature line for marketing purposes on EVERY email you send out.

    e. Create a promotion schedule for your services. Offering periodic discounts not only helps your client to save money, but it will bring in work that you might not have otherwise received.

    f. Ask clients to credit you for your work in the pieces that they publish, whether in print or online.

    g. Produce a yearly calendar in which the top page (the picture) features your work instead of photographs.

3. **Networking** – Yes. Again with the networking. It's important to the growth of your company that as many people as possible know who you are and what you do. Personally, I used to try to stay as anonymous as possible. Now, as a traveling writer, I make every attempt to be at as many functions as possible simply so that I can pass out business cards and other materials. Here's some ideas for you:

    a. Attend as many industry events as possible.

    b. Go to events that your target market may attend.

    c. Sponsor an event that your target market may attend.

    d. Again, join the local chamber of commerce.

    e. Do some pro-bono work for charitable organizations. They will give you credit for the work in most cases.

    f. Get involved in social groups like church school, colleges, etc.

g. Join industry organizations and get your name listed in their rosters.

h. Offer seminars to local business groups in which you can tell them how your work can benefit their company. Make use of industry-related online forums where you can work in what you do as part of the conversation.

i. Find industry-related blogs and comment on posts, adding in while doing so, the services that you offer. Stay professional and make sure everything is related.

4. **Promotions** – You'll soon find that every job you get is not a result of referrals or word of mouth. Clients will often find you by way of advertisements, directories and through marketing materials. You can help them to find these materials by doing one or more of the following:

a. Get magnetic signage for your car.

b. Have t-shirts made with your web address on the back and your logo on the front.

c. Use Google Adwords for internet advertising.

d. Advertise in industry-related magazines.

e. Make sure your company is listed in the Yellow Pages and other directories.

f. Research websites that your clients are most likely to use and then buy ad space on those sites.

g. Advertise in related online directories.

h. Advertise in your local newspaper's business section.

i. Participate in trade-shows

j. Use holiday greetings to place a line or two about your services.

k. Come up with a gimmick that makes you stand out from the crowd.

l. Give free advertising premiums with every consultation and in fact, make use of things like printed pens with your company name, web address and a tag line.

    m. Seek out industry newsletters and advertise within their pages.

5. **Become an expert within your target market** – Aligning yourself into a position as an expert will accomplish two things for you. First, it will bring you a lot more work. Second, you will be able to charge more for that work. You can become known as an industry expert in the following ways:

    a. Pitch an article to an industry publication.

    b. Repeat the same to industry blogs and resource websites.

    c. Offer to speak at industry events

    d. Create a blog on your website. In most cases, your blog can be your website.

    e. Submit tutorials and how-to papers to websites like Ezine Articles (www.ezinearticles.com) and other similar sites.

    f. Enter work that you do into competitions.

6. **Job Boards** – Many leads for freelance jobs are advertised, opening yet another avenue for you to find work. Bear in mind that you are still competing for work with other freelancers, but this is an avenue where you can and will get some of your work from as you are working on building your client list. As with anything else, you have to use due diligence when using job boards to find work. While the majority are legitimate offers, you have to beware of possible scammers as well. Here are some ideas:

    a. Search for job board websites to look for work.

    b. Craigslist *CAN* be a good source if you are careful.

    c. Use the job boards to place ads when you are looking for work.

    d. Utilize websites like upwork.com to find work

7. **Cold Calling** – Contacting companies out of the blue usually yields poor results, so don't go into this one thinking you are going to win a project with every call. In fact, you might not get any projects, or maybe even one out of every hundred calls. The most important thing though, is that you are letting people know that you are there.

a. Find out how you could improve a potential clients' business and profitability and then give them a "cold call" with a pitch that will set them thinking about why they never thought of that.
b. Mail postcards to potential clients.
c. Send promotional items to the potential client such as a calendar, pen, fun gadget, etc.

8. **Connect with local businesses**.
a. Contact companies like internet service providers or even printing companies and offer them commissions if they refer work to you. This is similar to the aforementioned affiliate program.
b. Make contact with companies like your own that is larger and may offer overflow work to you.
c. Contact other freelancers who may have taken on too much work themselves and perhaps they will slide some of it your way. This is a great opportunity to oversell your services and pass work on to others as well. BE CAREFUL THOUGH. Make sure their work is of the same quality or better than you offer or you may end up short a client due to shoddy work.
d. Cross promote your services with other businesses. This could be a potential win-win for you and a company that is not your competitor.
e. Check with local merchants to see if you can place business cards in their stores. You never know who might end up going into any given store, and especially fast food stores and convenience stores. You might just end up with multiple new clients who never knew of you.

HOW TO PRICE YOUR WORK

More often than not, you are going to quote prices to clients per project, or perhaps by the word. Still, you have to have an hourly cost to use as a basis for setting your prices. This is because you know that you need to make a certain amount of money each month to pay your bills. So, you have to price your work so that you are making at least that much per hour and more to cover overhead costs, plus a small percentage to earn a profit from your work for the company.

The first step in calculating your fees and your hourly rate is to determine how much you need to make each month to pay the bills. This is known as your break-even point. To do this, use the following steps:

1. **Calculate your personal costs** – How much money do you need each month to make it in the world? That means basically that you need to figure in housing, utilities, food, healthcare, car payments, etc.
2. **Calculate business expenses** – How much does it cost to run your business with things such as your office, utilities, phone service, internet, etc.
3. **Taxes and other liabilities** – Next you have to figure out the taxes you are going to have to pay. Other things you have to look at is your retirement fund, etc. Keep in mind that taxes are going to be relative to how much your company makes. The more income you have, the higher your taxes are going to be. As a general rule of thumb, and to stay on the safe side of the IRS man, once you have figured all your other costs, multiply that by 40% and you'll have a good starting spot for the taxes.

4. **Add it all together**. – the final sum is going to be the amount of money you are going to have to make each month just to break even.

5. **How Many Hours** – How many hours will you work for the year? The average person will work about 2000 hours per year, with two weeks figured in for vacation. If you want more vacation, then adjust that number accordingly. This will be used to determine the hourly rate you need to break even. The first mistake that every new freelancer makes is to assume that every hour from every working day is billable. It's not. Every hour you spend writing, is going to be followed by another hour of accounting and other paperwork. You'll also spend some of that time searching for or bidding on new work. Let's not forget time when you might be ill, and then there are holidays to consider as well. Also, there will be the dreaded "slow-period" when there will be no new work coming in.

6. **Divide costs by hours** – Now that you've done all of that, divide the total costs by the number of hours you came up with. First, take the total hours you came up with, then subtract the number of hours you want to set aside for vacation, the number of hours you want to set aside for holidays, and then the sick time. So let's say you came up with the same 2080 hours (40 hours a week X 52 weeks), and then take that 2080 hours and subtract 160 hours for vacation. That leaves you with 1920 hours. Let's say you have set aside five days for sick time, so we would subtract another 40 hours leaving you with 1880 hours. Now, let's look at only the big holidays. You may take more, or less, depending on your religion and other beliefs. NEW YEARS, MEMORIAL DAY, INDEPENDENCE DAY, LABOR DAY, THANKSGIVING DAY AND CHRISTMAS. Subtract another 48 hours from your total bringing you down to 1832 total hours. Now, you are actually going to be able to bill about half of those hours because remember, you are not writing every single hour available. This means that in this particular example, you are only going to be billing about 916 hours. So, take the totals of the amount that you need to simply break even and divide that total by 916. For our purposes, let's say that between household and business expenses, you figure out that you need $50,000 just to break even in the business. Take $50,000 and divide it by 916. You should come up with $54.00 and some change. That's what your break-even point is, and what you need to base your pricing on when giving clients quotes.

CALCULATING THE HOURLY RATE

Now that you have found your break-even point, we now have to calculate what your hourly rate should be, that will make your company one that is profitable.

1. **Profits** – The last section showed you the rate you need to charge that will help your company to break-even. No one however, is in business to simply break-even. The goal is to generate income above your break-even point. Profit you make is like putting money into a savings account. Part of your operating costs is your salary of course, but profit will help your company to grow in the end. So, consider it savings. The reality is that you will use some of this money to pay yourself when the work is lean. Of course, it will also cover business expense when the work is lean as well. Anything over and above that though, is money that you have saved. So, let's say that you decide that you want to save $20,000 over the course of the year. We need to add that to your hourly rate so that you can realize that savings. That said, take the $50,000 in business and living expenses that you came up with in the previous section. Add the $20,000 to it and your total is $70,000. Now divide that by the 916 billable hours that you found in the previous section. Your hourly rate has now grown to $76.00 and some change for every hour.

2. **Market Demand** – When your services are in high demand, you should consider charging even more for your services. There are some easy signs to determine whether or not your services are in high demand. First of all, if you have more work coming in than you can handle. On the other hand, if you find yourself in fierce competitions for work, then the demand for your services is not so high, and you'll have to consider adjusting your prices accordingly.

3. **The Industry Standard** – It's hard to figure out what others are charging for the same services you are offering. Most will not disclose this information, and your potential clients are not going to tell you either. Later on in the book, I offer a chart to give you an idea of what others are charging, but it's not an exact science because there are so many variables involved such as the quality of your work, customer service experiences, etc. Naturally, just starting out, you are not going to be known, so your earnings are going to be at the lower end of the scale, but it will at least give you an idea of where to start.

4. **Skill Levels** – Not every freelancer can deliver the same goods at the same quality, and clients expect prices to fluctuate accordingly. That said, every freelancer's hourly rate is going to be different. That said, when you are first starting out, you can expect to set your rates lower than those of your competitors. Your work may not be up to the standard of your competitors yet either. As you gain experience, there will be opportunities for that to change.

5. **Experience** – Though experience is generally bundled with skill levels, the reality is that experience is something completely different from skill. For example, you have two freelancers with the same skill. However, one freelancer recognizes the fact that he will have to do some extra research in order to complete a project, and he figures that into his quote. The other freelancer though, does not realize he will have to put in extra time for research. So he bids, not allowing for the time required to completely research his topic. He will ultimately lose money on the project, because he is not billing for the extra time needed on the subject at hand. Your pricing can also help the flow of clients to your business. Lower prices will generally mean more work while the higher prices will generally slow things down a little. So, you can use your prices to speed up incoming work or to slow it down.

6. **Business Strategy** – Strategy will also play a significant role in your pricing. Take a look at how you are pitching yourself and decide whether your prices are cheap and cheerful, high-end, or somewhere in between the two. It's a double-edged sword, really, when you think about it. If you price your services too low, people are going to wonder what's wrong, and if you price yourself too high, they are not going to inquire. There are several approaches then, to how to set prices. For example, you can simply settle on a rate you think is fair to you, and then double that to cover expenses and profit. Another thing that you could do, is to start of with low-ball prices and gradually up your rates as business grows. Low-rates generally work to get you repeat business and referrals. If you are doing good work, word will get around fast. The trouble however, is that you will have to work really hard to make ends meet at home and in the company. Then, as each new wave of clients approach you, raise prices just a little. You can level out once you reach an income level that you are happy with.

7. **Service** – The service you provide to clients will also play a huge factor in your pricing strategy. If you are a freelancer who will do what it takes 24/7/365 to get the job done, you are going to be able to command a higher price than your competitor.

8. **Maximums** –Sometimes, working as a freelancer lulls you into a state where you don't realize your true value as a service provider. When you take all things under consideration such as skill, experience and service, you may still be selling yourself short, and that means dollars out the window. At the end of the day, you should be pricing your services at the level that the market will bear. While all of this sounds confusing, the point is that you should be charging whatever your customers will pay without leaving you to go somewhere else. When I first started out, I charged 1 cent per word for website content. The work was incredibly easy and I could churn out most of the work because it was on topics that I knew a great deal about. I then started jacking my prices up every couple of months until I finally reached a point that I was getting $100.00 or more for a 500 word article. That's four times what I had set my hourly rate at back when I started. That said, the clients paying that kind of money were in the Fortune 500 zone. Small website owners aren't going to be able to afford that, but they should start be part of the mix to keep you working when you are starting out.

PRICE INCREASES

Your prices need to grow periodically to reflect the increasing costs around you. As you gain more experience and skill, you will be able to increase prices, albeit, gently. When you take on a client, charging a particular rate, the pricing for them should remain as such for a while. Let's say six months, the gently add an increase into the next quote you offer them. They will expect this, and if you keep it small, there will usually be no objections. You can also do it based on the number of projects you have done for them, say 15 or 20.

As you take on new clients however, price increases are easier to incorporate. When it comes to new clients though, you should be working in small increases for each new group of perhaps 10 or 15 clients. This will have your pricing all over the place it will seem, but it also gives you a chance to try to charge higher rates while still having clients at the lower rates, ensuring that there is still some income.

CHARGING BY THE JOB

Up to now, you've learned about the hourly rate. If you are like myself and most other freelancers, you will likely want to charge a flat rate for each project, page, etc. Here's how you can use your hourly rate to set prices for your flat rate projects.

1. Determine the amount of time that will be involved in completing the project. Once you know the scope of the project, you can translate that information into a total number of hours, based on what you know to be the number of hours needed to complete each page. For instance, if it's a topic I know about, I can turn out 10 pages of 500 words each in about two hours. I then use the hourly rate information that I have (let's say $76.00), and multiply that by two. In this case, that would be $152.00, or $15.20 per page.
2. In some cases, you will have to add to that quote, costs for rebilling as well. For example, so the client wants an image with each article. You have to pay for the image you get from the provider. This cost must be passed along to the customer as well, unless the cost for that item was very small. Rarely will you ever eat the cost, but on the other hand, providing the image at no cost to the client can be a way to gain even more work from them, or even referrals. In the case where you do bill the client for the image cost, you should also add an additional 25% as profit.
3. Now, let's say the cost is pretty high for the image that the client wants to use (I always use a stock photo place), then consider having the photographer (or service) to bill the client directly. This keeps your name from being attached to high costs.

Once you determine the price you wish to charge, you need to present it to the client. Before you do that, you need to understand that there are distinctive differences between what an estimate of charges is, as opposed a quote which is a statement of what will be charged for the project. With an estimate, the prices might be a little higher or lower than those stated on the form. With a quote, your client is going to expect to pay exactly that. I myself use quotes only. If a project is a little longer, or shorter, then so what? I want my client to know exactly what I am going to be charging them. In any case, you should itemize everything on the form so that the client will know what he's paying for.

CONTRACT TERMS AND CONDITIONS

A contract need not be anything fancy. It should however, spell out exactly what is expected between you and the client. Some freelancers choose to use formal contracts. That's fine, but I don't and I haven't had any problems in 14 years. However, I do use the quote as the agreement, and require that I receive a signed copy in return before I start work, unless I am have extensive documentation through a third party website such as Upwork.com.

The terms and conditions are basic, but when spelled out in the quote and signed by the client, it constitutes a contract. Some of the terms should be:

1. When will the invoice come due? I typically ask for payment up front with new clients. If I am working through a third-party site, they will collect the money and hold it in escrow until completion of the work and acceptance by the client. Older clients who have been with me a while can be billed. You have to be careful though. Don't let a client's bill climb too high. You've done the work, so you need to be paid. You have to eat too, right?
2. How should rebilling items be handled? Is everything going to fall under your invoice, or will the other provider send their own bill.
3. Do you require a deposit before work begins.
4. Who owns the copyright on the completed work? In most cases, at least when writing for the web, your work will be work for hire, and all rights convey to the client. The same is true in the case of magazines, except the difference will usually be higher pay, plus you get to keep the byline. The contract should spell everything out so that at the end of the day, there is no confusion.
5. Ownership of the work before completion of the project. Rights do not typically take place until after a client accepts and pays for the project. Anything short of that, and the work still belongs to me. If for some reason they do not buy the work, or they stiff me on the fee (that has happened), then I will use the work elsewhere, such as at the article banks, or on a site like ezinearticles.com
6. Finally, it should spell out your rights and responsibilities as well as those of the client.

RETAINERS AND REGULAR GIGS

Not every job will be a one-time thing. In this case, the client may ask that you charge a retainer fee so that they can secure your services for ongoing projects. This might mean producing work on a regular basis for a blog or website or for some other type of work. This is the best type of job to have, because in its simplest form, it means ongoing, steady work for you. When you have a client on retainer, you might consider charging lower rates to them in view of the fact that the work will be consistent.

TOO CHEAP, TOO EXPENSIVE

Personally, I have never heard a client say that a quote was too cheap. However, you might put in a bid on work and undersell yourself, thereby losing money. Other times, you may quote a price that the client considers too high. Let's look at both:

1. Being too cheap is not usually a problem. In some cases however, the client might wonder why your work is so cheap. However, in most cases, you will be simply selling yourself short. Regular clients may often joke about how cheap your prices are, or they might thank you for such a great deal. Keep your ears open. You're leaving money on the table if you are underselling yourself. Another thing is pricing yourself too cheap by underestimating the amount of work that is actually involved in getting the job done. We run into a problem as freelancers inasmuch as we want the work badly enough that we are afraid to quote a price that is too high, but in any case, when you figure out you are underselling yourself, to to increase the quote on the next project to make up for it. It's really not ethical, and in fact, may even anger your client if you try to increase pricing once a quote has been given. The bottom line is to learn from your mistakes, and then move on.
2. Too expensive can also be a problem because it will lose work for you. If you find that you are no longer gaining new clients or referrals, then the first thing you will need to look at is your pricing strategy. One way of finding out you are trying to charge too much, is to consider each meeting with a client. If they are extremely interested in your work, but fail to call you back when you submit the quote, then perhaps the pricing is the deciding factor for them.

If there is the possibility that the prices are too high, then consider the fact that you may have to lower your prices, but increase working hours in order to make the bills. Remember the fact that while there are a number of factors to consider with setting prices, bear in mind that the economy will have its say so on the matter as well.

It's a fine line between what will work and what won't. There's a fine balance, and you have to find out where that balance is. One way of doing this, is to quote your price, and if the client feels that the price is too high, you can try negotiating to get your foot in the door. Just keep in mind when you do that the client is going to work to get the price down as low as they can. In one project, I placed a bid to a client at one cent per word, or $5.00 for a 500 word article. The client then came back to me that the cost was too high. In the end, he wanted me to work at a rate of $1.00 per 500 words, or in my case, about $4.00 an hour (I can get 500 words about every 15 minutes when I know the topic). The terms of the project that the guy demanded, was a writer whose first language was English and was from the United States. There is no one in the U.S. who can live on that, regardless of where you live, so of course, I turned him down. The point of this story is that you are going to lose some jobs over clients who want to pay too little. Move on to the next one who is willing to pay what you are worth. The other guys are just trying to get something for nothing.

In the next section of the book, we are going to discuss project timing.`

PROJECT TIMING

EXPECTATIONS

From the start, expectations of yourself and your client need to be documented. When you set these expectations, there can be no confusion about any aspect of the project in question. There are two parts to this – the first part must spell out what is expected of the project itself and the second half will detail how you and the client will work together until the project is complete.

1. Before you actually begin on the project, there must be an agreement between you and the client about the work you will produce. Every detail must be documented, and you have to ensure that you both share the same vision of the completed project. You have to ensure that both parties have the same goals in mind. These details are usually nailed down during the briefing meeting, or if you are primarily dealing with clients online, it actually gets a little easier because all of the details can be hammered out in the emails that you are sending back and forth to one another. Now is the time to be asking any questions that you may have. If you find that there are still questions, pick up the phone and give the client a call, or shoot them off an email with all questions that you may still have.

2. Just as important as it is that you nail down all details of the project itself, are the details of how you and the client will work together. Will you simply complete the project and submit it to the client for approval or is there a period of revision? Will the client check in with you periodically to see the rough draft as you work on it? Most of your clients will know that feedback is expected when the project is completed, but there are a few who will expect to "be right there" as the work is going on. Personally, I don't like that aspect, because it only serves to slow me down, but each client is different. Make sure that each party knows what is expected before the project begins. I had one client who insisted on a phone call every day on the premise of just checking to see how things were going. This actually translated into lost work of at least an hour, sometimes much more because of idle chit-chat. This means a loss of money because those are working hours you will not get back. When I tried to explain to the client that these calls were taking me away from his project, he took offense. In the end, I ended up backing out of the project because it was getting to a point where I was actually losing money on it, relative to time lost. You need to decide where you are going to draw the line on such shenanigans, but understand too that the more time spent on the phone, the less money you will make. Especially considering that only half of your day's hours are actually going to be billable.

At the end of the day, the work agreement must spell out the scope of the project, the expectations from you and the client, what the final deliverables will be and the timeframe in which the final product will be delivered. By all means, always make sure that you deliver that final product on or before the day it is due. In as many cases as possible, it should be delivered before the due date to allow for any necessary changes.

TRACK YOUR HOURS

For at least the first two years you are in business, it is extremely important that you track every hour you work, and by work, I mean actually writing. There are a number of apps on the market today for use on computers, cell phones, tablets, etc. When you start writing, you hit a button, when you are through writing, you hit the button again. These apps also let you specify the exact project you are working on, so you can refer back later to see the amount of time you actually spend on a particular project.

Back when you figured out the details of the project, you should have allowed a little time for any changes that may need to be made. That' why it's so important that you complete a project as quickly as possible, and then you will have any necessary time to make those changes before the deadline comes.

When you own your own business, there is nothing worse than to feel like you accomplished nothing at day's end. Worse still, is not understanding what happened to make you feel that way. That's why it's important to track your hours spent writing. On the other hand, perhaps it's best that you track hours spent doing other, non-writing work as well. Learning to understand where your day goes will help you to become more productive, so that you feel like you have actually accomplished something.

RECORD KEEPING

You've already learned that there are a variety of ways to stay in touch with your clients and for tracking your time, etc. Now let's talk about record keeping. You should be logging every conversation you have with clients, note any changes they make to the project(s) you are working on, etc.

Keep minutes of any meetings you have, whether in person or on the phone. Keep all records safe. They can be electronic if you wish, which is actually better because paperwork would have to be stored somewhere. With electronic records, you can save everything to a thumb drive or an SD card, or even a CD. (Thumb drives are best). The same thing goes with emails. Save them to the thumb drive for later retrieval if necessary.

What I usually do, is have a hierarchy of folders in my documents section. The main folder indicates that it is my client information, and then inside that I have a folder for each client. Inside the client folders, I have folders for emails, project information, meeting notes, etc.

You can even use a project management application if your budget allows such an expense at startup. You can Google search for such software to find the many titles available. It would be useless to list everything here because things change so fast and the information is likely to change at some point, perhaps even before this book is published.

The hardest part of using such applications, is getting your client to actually login to the interface to use it, but if you do, everything can be handled within it including the customer contacting you, "online meetings", uploading and downloading files, etc. and everything will have date and time stamps.

REVISIONS

Be prepared at any given time to make revisions to your projects for the client. It doesn't happen often, but when you bid a project, you should include some time for the revisions as well. The hardest part of planning for such things is getting the number of times a client will want revisions correct. Still, in the end it all balances out. You can safely assume two revisions and then leave it at that. What I typically do, is notify the client when I place my bid that I will allow up to two revisions to the work, based on his or her feedback. Anything after that and it becomes billable. Some clients can be really nitpicky, so you want to be flexible for that repeat business, but you can't let it get out of hand either, so learn how to be just as firm as you are flexible. If the client is too troublesome and ends up costing you more money than you are making, then once the project is complete, you can consider whether or not it is worth the effort to take any further work from them.

BUDGET AND TIMELINE BLOWOUTS

You will, from time to time run into situations where you will blow the budget. There are only two reasons that this will ever happen:

1. The problem is your fault – usually because you underestimated how much was actually involved in the project. It can also happen however because the tasks were completed incorrectly, or there was some other error made. In any case, you have to eat the loss. It was your fault. No big deal. It happens sometimes. I've been in the business for more than 14 years and it still happens to me occasionally.

2. Client's fault – If the client didn't communicate properly to you exactly what was needed, or didn't deliver material that you needed to complete the project, or maybe even they are requesting too many revisions, then it falls into the category of being their fault. Perhaps the client doesn't fully comprehend what's involved, or they are overly excited about the project and begin making changes too early in the game. Whatever the reason is, it's your job to control everything so that it doesn't get out of hand. This is the point in time when you need that paper outlining the details of the project, that the client signed (hopefully). This shows them what they agreed to. It also shows the the amount of time you estimated the project would take, and how much more time they are actually adding to the project. When they do this, you need to let them know that you need to be fairly compensated for the extra work they have created. As you begin to gain more experience, you will start to notice the signs that this is about to happen and you will be able to warn the client early. Some will be happy to pay any additional costs when it comes to something that was their fault, many will not. You have to be firm, or you will end up performing work, free of charge, and the bill collectors do not want to hear it. In some cases, a dispute may arise over the situation, but whatever else happens, always stay professional and don't lose your cool.

OVERDELIVERING

When you go above and beyond, delivering more to the client than they paid for. It might be some sort of copy written that they never asked you to deliver or something along those lines. In any case, that's great. They'll love you for it, but be careful in doing so. If you do it too often however, they will come to expect it all of the time, and that's a can of worms you just don't want to open. So yes, by all means do this once in a while, but do so sparingly.

On another note, sometimes the client will run up against their own deadline, and they will have some piece of work that needs completed that no one else can get done, so you step in and save the day for them. You'll be a hero, and this goes a long way to build client loyalty. Again, this is something that you want to be careful with, because you may have other clients that you are serving, and they will begin to consistently ask you to save the day for them, and it will hinder your customer service to other clients.

81

COLLECTING YOUR FEES

INVOICING

An invoice is the bill you send to the client for the work you completed. There are a number of ways you can generate an invoice including handwriting or typing it, through an accounting program, or even using Microsoft Word or Excel.

There are even web applications that you can use, with payment collection systems such as PayPal, credit cards, etc built in to the system. An invoice should typically include the following information at a minimum:

1. An invoice number
2. Your Logo
3. Your Company Name
4. Your Company Address
5. Your Business tax ID number
6. The Clients Name and Address
7. Details revolving around the project
8. Itemized detailing of the charges
9. Any taxes payable such as Sales Tax if required in your jurisdiction
10. Total amount due
11. Your payment terms

PAYMENT TERMS

Payment terms, in its simplest form, is when you expect the client to pay the bill. For example:

1. **Within X number of days** – usually these terms will be seen as net 10, or net 30, meaning that the client must pay the bill within that timeframe. Many businesses offer something like a 2% discount if the invoice is paid before the due date. In such cases, you may see 2% 10/Net 30 which means the client may deduct 2% from the bill if they pay it before the 10th day. Otherwise, the invoice is due in 30 days.
2. **Cash on Delivery** – this means that the invoice must be paid before the work is delivered to the client.
3. **Prior to delivery** – is essentially the same thing as cash on delivery.

You should make it as easy as possible for your client to pay you. Most freelancers offer to accept credit cards. Some also accept payment systems like Paypal or something similar. Most also take checks. Taking checks should not be much of a problem, but you may run into issues, and it will depend on local laws on how to collect on bounced checks, and it's beyond the scope of this book to get into all of that. If this does happen to you, and as I said, it's rare, then check with your local courthouse to see what can be done about it.

Accepting credit cards is easier than ever these days. You should always offer to accept payment in the form of a credit card or bank card if it has the Visa or Mastercard logo.

You should be aware that when you are working for a major corporation, they have their own payment systems in place, and it is common for them to wait 60 or even 90 days to get paid. The upside of this is that while it may take some time to get your money, you can usually rest assured that you will in fact be paid. Your payment terms should be part of the work agreement. Always.

DEPOSITS AND MILESTONES

It is a good idea to ask for a deposit before you begin working on the project. This will lessen the risk you take in spending time and effort on a client who you may not yet trust. Deposits are typically between 10% and 50% of the final amount payable.

If you do ask for a deposit, send the client an invoice for it prior to your starting work on the project. Be sure to state on the invoice that work will begin once the deposit has been paid. You should also state the circumstances under which a full or partial refund will be possible. Possible scenarios might be if you are unable to work on the project due to illness or some other unforeseen circumstance, or if the project as a whole is cancelled for some reason before work has begun. It is up to you to define the terms, but having them on the invoice will give your client peace of mind that they will see their money again if you cannot fulfill your part of the deal for some reason.

Likewise, if the project is large and you want payments at various milestones, an invoice should be sent accordingly. Naturally, you will not proceed to the next milestone before payment is received for the milestone you have just completed.

CASH FLOW

You'll see the term cash flow a lot during the course of conducting business. It is a simple term, but very important in concept. Without cash flow, you'll not be able to pay any bills. What the term cash flow refers to is the money that comes into your business and flows out. In its simplest form, it means you collecting your fees and then paying the bills.

When you reach a point where a lot of money is flowing into your company and not as much going out, you'll be in great shape. It takes time for that to start happening on a regular basis though. In your line of work, you will typically be primarily billing for work that you have already completed. In some cases, it may take a while to be paid for that work meaning that at any given time you will be waiting for money to come in from clients.

The problem is that having money owed to you does not equal having it in your account. After all, you cannot pay your bills with invoices, so you are going to need that money that the invoices represent. When it comes time to pay the bills, if that money is still on paper and not in the bank, it represents a cash flow problem.

In your regular day job, your time card represented you invoice, and your employer paid you every week (or two weeks). Your client however, may take 30 or more days to pay you. You'll find that you have some weeks where the cash os flowing nicely, and others where you are still waiting on payments to come in. To make things even worse, you may not have any new work coming in either. It is essential therefore, that you plan ahead of time for these instances.

When cash is flowing nicely, pay your bills, and yourself. Don't look at the extra cash as a windfall and simply run out spending the money. That needs to stay in your bank account for the eventual cash flow/slow work problems. That way, you can still collect a paycheck and pay your bills. It's as simple as that.

It's for that reason, that I previously told you to work out what you need to sustain your household each month, and to sustain your business expenses each month.

This means establishing a budget for both the home and the company, and then sticking to it. Don't forget that you will also need a cash reserve for the various taxes that you will have to pay, because all of those bills must be paid, whether your clients are paying you or not.

When you do create your budgets, add an extra 20% to that for contingency. If a contingency never arises, then that money can go to savings. Understand that all the while, these budgets will not make your clients pay you any faster. They just give you an idea of what you are going to need at the beginning of each month to live.

The thing is, if you begin your company in January, you can be reasonably certain that you may not start receiving any month for a month, maybe even two months, in fact. That's one of the reasons it's so important that you have money set aside to live on as you build your company. The blow is lessened a little if you have a spouse that works a regular job, not so much if you are both working the freelance scene and just starting out.

As that cash starts to come in, don't waste it. Pay yourself and the bills and leave the rest alone, at least until you have enough to sustain both yourself and the company for at least three months. More in fact, if possible.

GET AN ACCOUNTANT

Maybe not right at the beginning, but sometime soon after opening your company, you need to start looking for an accountant that you can trust. An accountant will be able to explain to you the various taxes and other costs that you are responsible for. The accountant will also be able to recommend a good computer program for bookkeeping for daily use within your business. If you hire a bookkeeper, they can maintain the books for you on a daily basis. The accountant does not do your daily record keeping but instead, does things like make sure your books are correct, file your periodic taxes, etc.

I'm not making a recommendation one way or the other, but in my business, I use quickbooks to do may daily bookkeeping. I have also taken some accounting classes, so I file my own tax forms and such, but unless you are well-versed in the tax laws and such, I wouldn't recommend that you do that. My workdays actually end up being anywhere from 12-15 hours because I do much of it myself. I do much of it myself because I travel a lot. On the other side of that coin, I also have plenty of time to do what I want to do as well, but then I have been doing this for 14++ years too.

DAILY BOOKKEEPING

It's extremely important to the growth of the company, and to your cash flow that you keep meticulous records. Do the bookkeeping every day that you have something to enter, or it will simply pile up. You will need to keep copies of all incoming receipts, outgoing receipts, taxes paid, etc. Do not mix business funds with personal funds. In fact, even if you are a sole-proprietor, you should still have a separate business bank account. When you pay yourself, write a check from the business account and deposit it into your personal account. This maintains the necessary records when it comes time to present them to your accountant for his annual audits and tax filings.

If you have petty cash in the office for minor expenses, use petty cash slips to document every penny you spend and it should include what you spent the money on when you do use it. Save those slips. Every scrap of paper showing your finances and how you used the money will come in handy not only for your accountant, but also in case your company is audited for any reason. Keep everything up to date when changes occur. Don't put anything of until the last minute.

The same thing holds true when you pay bills, make charitable contributions, etc because these are tax deductible items. Otherwise, if you are not able to account for it, you will be taxed for it, potentially losing you money. Take the time to learn from your accountant what is and is not tax deductible. This can work to keep more money in your accounts.

ACCEPTING PAYMENTS

I already touched on this some, but it's important enough to mention again. Make it as easy as possible for your clients to pay you. Accept credit/debit cards, Paypal, and accept checks. If you have international clients, then perhaps credit/debit cards and Paypal are the best choices. Whatever methods you do decide to accept, be aware that there will usually be fees involved.

Whether you are paying credit card processing fees, Paypal fees, or the monthly charge that your bank charges you to maintain your account with them. Some banks even limit the number of transactions you can make each month with business accounts. If you have checks coming in on a daily basis, bundle them and make deposits once a week instead of daily (unless you have large sums coming in).

GETTING CLIENTS TO PAY

Unfortunately, during your freelancing career, you, just like other businesses, are going to run into one or more clients who either refuse to pay for your services, there will be those who try to pay you a reduced amount, or they will simply put off paying you for as long as they possibly can. This can create a significant problem as far as cash flow is concerned. This is especially true if the project was large and represents a significant portion of your income for a certain period. This only serves to reiterate why it is important that you have cash reserves on hand to cover the bills.

That one seemingly small problem is the reason why many small businesses shut their doors prematurely. Just think, one client can be responsible for shutting down your entire operation before you have the chance to grow the company.

To start with, it's always good to have clear itemized quotes, that have been signed and accepted by the client. The paper trail I talked about earlier, and all of the documentation as well, all play a huge part in your business, so don't shirk on it. It's also important that the invoice have a clear date of when it is due. The net 30, and other wording like that will cover it in this case.

When a client is taking too long to pay, you can send them a friendly reminder that payment is past due. Don't be embarrassed to send them such a notice. In fact, if anyone should be embarrassed about the situation, it's the client. You've stood by the terms and you've done your part. Now it's time for them to step up, do the right thing, and pay the bill.

In most cases, a single reminder will do the trick and the payment will follow. If a client gets annoyed when you remind them to pay you, then you can probably take that as a hint that they are trying to avoid paying the bill at all. If that is actually the case, then in the end they are a client that you will be better off without.

One thing, and this is just a suggestion. Some use while others don't, but you can institute a system of charging a late fee for overdue payments. I do this to the tune of 1.5% per month the bill is overdue, and the late fee is added to the principal. If it continues through to the next month, the late fee is added again and so on. The key here is that you clearly state on the invoice that there is a late fee added to each invoice, and that will generally deter late payments.

For the client that is trying to reduce the payment in some way, there is a similar, but slightly different approach. First, the invoicing is the same, but when the client is trying to pay you less than the amount agreed upon, then you contact them and ask them if there was a problem with the work. The important thing is that you not get aggressive about the situation. If they have a legitimate issue, then perhaps adjustments can be made, but if not, you need to try to convince them that the bill needs to be paid. All of your documentation about the project will come in handy here as well.

If they still refuse to pay the balance, then you have to consider possibly dropping them from your client list. It all depends on a number of different variables, and only you can decide whether or not they are worth keeping in the Rolodex. Clients are hard to come by, but if they aren't paying their bills as agreed, then you're losing anyway.

If a client outright refuses to pay the bill, then you have to consider legal action. This is much easier if they are local, not so much if they are in a different state (this is where having an attorney is helpful). You can always consider reporting non-payment to the credit bureaus, both business and personal if they are not incorporated, business only if they are.

Of course, that doesn't get you paid, but they may not want the black mark on their record either. From there, you can consider submitting the invoice to a debt collector, but they will take a significant piece of the collection for their efforts, however, some money in a case like this is better than no money. In many cases, when a client refuses to pay, a threat of legal action will generally motivate them.

Beyond that, if the amount is less than $500.00, you're probably better off writing the debt off and treating it as a lesson learned. The new tax laws in effect now allow you to submit a 1099 to those who have bad debts with you, and the government taxes the debt as income for them. I'm sketchy on the details with this particular situation, so contact your accountant to determine how something like that works.

Now, with all of that being said, the good news that the vast majority of your clients will pay their bills on time, every time so don't let any of this worry you right now, however, you need to understand that it is always a possibility that someone may not pay.

JOHN E DEROSSETT

EXPANDING YOUR SERVICE

Most people are perfectly happy to be a freelancer, take on as much work as they can handle themselves, and they are content. Others however, look at their company as something that they want to grow, eventually having others to do the work for them, or simply hiring others to make the company bigger. For myself, I'm content to make the money that I need to live on, and to put a little in savings.

There are different ways that you can grow your company including hiring in-house employees, or by simply subcontracting the work to others.

SUBCONTRACTING

When you get a project from your client, you are the contractor. If you pass it along to someone else for one reason or another, then you are subcontracting the work. Even if you are content to have your business the way it is, there will almost always come a point in time where you will have to pass a project along to someone else.

One of the ways this might happen is if you take on more work than you can handle. You might have to hire a subcontractor in order to meet deadlines.

Another time when you may need to hire a subcontractor is when you end up with a project that includes something that you cannot do yourself. Not to worry though. There are some benefits to subcontracting work to others, and we'll talk about those in a few minutes. The first thing I need to hit on though, is to warn you about working with people that you do not know.

You have to vet other writers carefully. If you don't, then you may end up running into quality problems. When you hire a subcontractor, check their portfolio. Give them a small writing project that you will pay them for, and then check their work carefully. In any case, the benefits of subcontracting work to others.

1. You have an opportunity to increase your income. If you bid the job, and then offer the subcontractor less for the project, you can earn more money. After all, you were the one that secured the job, and the subcontractor might not have had a project to do had you not found that work.
2. Next, if you subcontract, then you do not have to turn away work, essentially sending a client elsewhere. When you know you are going to need to hire a subcontractor, price the work a little higher, and then pass along extra earnings to the subcontractor while still making money yourself.
3. Next, taking on subcontractors is a stepping stone to growing your company. You can essentially take on much more work than you otherwise would have.

The important thing here, is that when you have a subcontractor, or many subcontractors, always make sure that you read everything over before sending it on to your client. This way, you know you are getting quality work to your client, and if it's less than stellar, you can make edits where necessary before sending it on.

Now, it's important that you don't let the benefits blind you here. There are also drawbacks when you hire subcontractors, and a couple have already been mentioned.

1. Remember to carefully vet all new subcontractors.
2. Remember to check all work before submitting it to the client.
3. You have to be able to pay the subcontractor, even though you have not yet been paid.
4. You may end up losing the client anyway. The client hired you because they like your work. It's possible that they may realize that you did not in fact do the project yourself, and they may move on to someone else. Most of the time this will not happen, but it's best to understand that this is always a possibility.

When you turn a project over to a subcontractor, it's important that he or she know the full scope of the project, and exactly what is expected of them. There's no sense in hiring a subcontractor to begin with, if you end up having to do the project over yourself to make sure it's right.

Always make sure the subcontractor gives you his or her quote before you send a quote off to the client. There's two reasons for this. First of all, you don't want to under-quote and lose money on the deal, which in turn gives the other reason, and that's to make sure that you can make some money from the deal too. It's the way business works. In all cases, it is important that the subcontractor understand that you are the boss, and that the way you want things done is the only way they are to be done. It's your client, and you have to protect their interests as well. If the subcontractor cannot or will not adhere to this, then it's time to search for another to fill his or her place.

RESOURCES

Now, earlier on, I promised some resources to help you get started in finding work. The resources section basically consists of a listing of some places that you can find some work to tide you over as you work on building your client list. I have also added some magazines that you may want to pitch article ideas to in order to find work that way as well.

PLACES TO FIND WORK ONLINE

Upwork – a freelancer marketplace where you bid against others to get writing jobs, or just about any other type of job a freelancer of any profession can do
http://www.upwork.com

Zerys Content Solutions – you apply for work here and once accepted, you can choose from any of the jobs offered in the project dashboard. Work isn't plentiful because of the number of writers there, but you can usually be paid halfway decent. It's a good place to get work if things are slow.
http://www.zerys.com

Craigslist is a place where you can sometimes find writing work, but as always, beware of who you are dealing with on sites

like this. Unfortunately, you may end up with someone trying to get free work out of you more often than not.
http://www.craigslist.org

Freelance Writing is another marketplace where you can find some work. I don't know much about this one, but I hear good things.
http://www.freelancewriting.com

The Write Life is another source that can point you in the right direction for finding work.
http://www.thewritelife.com

Outsource is sort of like Upwork.
http://www.outsource.com

Finally, one I know very little about, is Freelanced. It's a social network for freelancers that also has job listings.
http://www.freelanced.com

MAGAZINES

When you write for magazines, it's sometimes difficult to get them to accept your pitches. Unless you have some experience at writing, and you have some stuff published under your name or online, it's going to be difficult to get them to even read your pitch. Nonetheless, I have included some of them here so you can take a shot at contacting if and when you feel ready.

1. Entrepreneur Magazine; queries@entrepreneur.com; $1.00/word
2. American Baby Magazine; abletters@americanbaby.com
3. The Atlantic Monthly; submissions@theatlantic.com
4. The New Yorker; www.newyorker.com; find contact info on the website
5. Fitness Magazine;fitquestions@fitnessmagazine.com
6. American Craft; mmoses@craftcouncil.org;
7. Dollhouse Miniatures; auralea@ashdown.co.uk

8. Model Cars Magazine; Gregg@modelcarsmag.com
9. Quilting Arts Magazine; submissions@quiltingarts.com
10. The American Gardener; editor@ahs.org
11. Atlanta Homes and Lifestyles; editor@atlantahomesmag.com
12. House Beautiful; readerservices@housebeautiful.com
13. Mountain Living; greatideas@mountainliving.com
14. This Old House; toh_letters@thisoldhouse.com
15. Boys Life; www.boyslife.org. Check website for contact info.
16. Cricket Magazine; www.cricketmag.com; Check website for contact info
17. Girl's Life; writerforgl@girlslife.com
18. Jack and Jill; jackandjill@uskidsmags.com
19. Ellery Queen's Mystery Magazine; elleryqueenmm@dellmagazines.com
20. Wired Magazine; submit@wired.com

There are of course, thousands of more magazines on the market, many dealing with specialized niches. Google can help with some, but your absolute best resource for contacting other magazines is to subscribe to Writer's Market at http://www.writersmarket.com

I have absolutely no connection with any of the sites that I have listed on these pages. Many are resources I have used, and I simply thought I would pass the information along.

I do intend to update this book as things change. For those of you who purchase the book for Kindle on Amazon, when I update the book, you will have the opportunity to get the free update.

ABOUT THE AUTHOR

John is an avid dog lover and has a nomadic spirit. In 2016 John and his wife Marlene decided to act on that spirit to hit the open road and full-time RV living as John continues to pursue his writing career.

While capable of writing about just about any subject, John focuses his effort on online business and is an expert in affiliate program marketing, online business, freelancing and retail.

He has since decided to share what he has learned over the last 14 years with others. Starting a Freelance Writing Business is the first of a series of books planned by John geared toward helping those that are new to the internet and entrepreneurial world.